FOOD LOVERS

THE FAMILY COOKBOOK

Trans
Atlantic
Press

All recipes serve four people, unless otherwise indicated.

For best results when cooking the recipes in this book, buy fresh ingredients and follow the instructions carefully. Make sure that everything is properly cooked through before serving, particularly any meat and shellfish, and note that as a general rule vulnerable groups such as the very young, elderly people, pregnant women, convalescents and anyone suffering from an illness should avoid dishes that contain raw or lightly cooked eggs.

For all recipes, quantities are given in standard U.S. cups and imperial measures, followed by the metric equivalent. Follow one set or the other, but not a mixture of both because conversions may not be exact. Standard spoon and cup measurements are level and are based on the following:

1 tsp. = 5 ml, 1 tbsp. = 15 ml, 1 cup = 250 ml / 8 fl oz.

Note that Australian standard tablespoons are 20 ml, so Australian readers should use 3 tsp. in place of 1 tbsp. when measuring small quantities.

The electric oven temperatures in this book are given for conventional ovens with top and bottom heat. When using a fan oven, the temperature should be decreased by about 20–40°F / 10–20°C – check the oven manufacturer's instruction book for further guidance. The cooking times given should be used as an approximate guideline only.

CONTENTS

SOUPS AND SAUCES

Tomato Soup
with Vegetables

Ingredients

2 carrots, finely chopped

1 stalk of celery, sliced

4 tbsp olive oil

2 cloves garlic, finely chopped

4 scallions (spring onions), finely chopped

4 oz / 100 g string beans, topped and tailed and chopped

2 small zucchini (courgettes), finely chopped

2 cups / 400 g canned tomatoes, chopped

3½ cups / 800 ml vegetable broth (stock)

1 bay leaf

1 sprig of thyme

1 tbsp tomato paste

½ cup / 100 g chick peas (garbanzo beans), canned, drained

⅓ cup / 30 g freshly shaved Parmesan cheese

A few fresh basil leaves, to garnish

Method

Prep and cook time: 50 min

1. Fry the carrots and celery in hot olive oil for around 3 minutes, add the garlic, scallions (spring onions), string beans, zucchini (courgettes) and tomatoes and continue frying for a further 1–2 minutes.

2. Add the broth (stock), bay leaf and thyme, season with salt and pepper and stir in the tomato paste. Simmer gently for a further 10–15 minutes.

3. Add the chick peas and simmer for 5 minutes until cooked through.

4. To serve, ladle into bowls, scatter with Parmesan cheese and garnish with basil leaves.

Carrot and Orange Soup

Ingredients

2 tbsp butter

1 onion, chopped

6 carrots, peeled and grated

1 potato, baking, peeled and grated

2½ cups / 600 ml vegetable broth (stock)

2 oranges, grated zest and juice

2 tbsp crème fraîche

Dash port wine (optional)

Pinch cayenne pepper

2 tbsp fresh parsley, chopped

Salt & freshly milled pepper

Method

Prep and cook time: 30 min

1. Sauté the chopped onion in hot butter, add the grated carrots and potato, season with salt, cover and cook for about 5 minutes.

2. Now pour in enough vegetable broth (stock) so that the vegetables are covered. Add the orange zest, cover and simmer for a further 10 minutes.

3. Purée the soup until smooth. Add the orange juice and the crème fraîche and stir. Pour in a little vegetable stock, depending on the thickness of the soup.

4. Season to taste with port wine, salt and cayenne pepper. Garnish with chopped parsley and freshly milled pepper and serve.

Pea Soup with Crème Fraîche

Ingredients

1 shallot

1 clove garlic

1 tbsp butter

$2^2/_3$ cups / 400 g frozen peas

1 tsp ginger, freshly grated

$2\frac{1}{2}$ cups / 600 ml chicken broth (stock)

Scant ½ cup / 100 ml whipping cream

Salt & freshly milled pepper

2 tbsp crème fraîche

Method
Prep and cook time: 20 min

1 Peel and finely chop the shallot and garlic. Heat the butter and sauté the shallot and garlic, then add the peas and ginger. Stir in the chicken broth (stock) and bring to a boil.

2 Simmer the soup for 6–8 minutes, then add the cream and purée the soup finely. Push through a sieve if you wish.

3 Season to taste with salt and pepper and ladle into bowls. Add a swirl of crème fraîche to each and serve.

Garlic Soup with Bread

Ingredients

12 cloves garlic

1 sprig sage

$4\frac{1}{4}$ cups /1 liter vegetable broth (stock)

2 tbsp olive oil

2 bay leaves

1 cup /100 g grated Parmesan cheese

2 egg yolks

2 tbsp whipping cream

Salt & freshly milled pepper

2 tbsp sherry

1 tbsp lemon juice

1 tbsp mustard

4 toasted baguette slices

Fresh parsley, to garnish

Method
Prep and cook time: 30 min

1. Peel the garlic and wash the sage leaves. Put into a pan with the vegetable broth (stock), bay leaves and olive oil and bring to a boil. Simmer, half-covered with a lid, for 15 minutes.

2. Take out the bay leaves and sage and purée the soup with a hand blender.

3. Mix the Parmesan cheese, egg yolks and cream.

4. Remove the soup from the heat and carefully stir in the cheese mixture. Season with salt and pepper and add sherry, lemon juice and mustard to taste.

5. Ladle the soup into 4 soup bowls and add a toasted baguette slice to each. Serve garnished with garlic and the parsley.

Chilled Tomato Soup
with Croûtons

Ingredients

2¼ lb / 1 kg tomatoes

1 onion

3 cloves garlic

1 bunch parsley

1 bunch basil

2 sprigs thyme

1 sprig savory

2 tbsp olive oil

Salt & freshly milled pepper

2 slices rye bread

3 tbsp butter, to fry

Method

Prep and cook time: 1 hour plus 1 hour refrigeration time

1. Wash, quarter and de-seed the tomatoes. Peel and quarter the onion and garlic.

2. Put the tomatoes into a blender with the chopped herbs, onion, garlic and salt and blend.

3. Push through a sieve if you wish. Season to taste with salt and pepper.

4. Stir in the olive oil and chill in the refrigerator for at least an hour.

5. Dice the bread, fry in butter and scatter over the soup before serving.

Creamy Leek and Pea Soup

Ingredients

2 leeks

1 clove garlic

1 lettuce

2 oz / ½ stick / 50 g butter

1 tsp chopped thyme leaves

4 cups / 1 liter chicken or vegetable broth (stock)

1¾ cups / 300 g frozen peas

1 tbsp chopped mint leaves

1¹/₃ cups / 300 g whipping cream

Salt & freshly milled pepper

Croutons, to garnish

Method

Prep and cook time: 25 min

1. Wash and trim the leeks and cut into rings. Peel and chop the garlic. Wash and shred the lettuce.

2. Heat the butter in a pan and sauté the leeks, thyme and garlic. Add the broth (stock) and bring back to a boil. Add the peas and lettuce and simmer gently for 5–6 minutes, until the peas are soft.

3. Remove from the heat and purée finely. Add the mint and cream and return to a boil. Season with salt and pepper and serve scattered with croutons

Spicy Corn Cream Soup
with Fried Bacon

Ingredients

10 oz / 280 g can of corn kernels

1 onion, diced

2½ cups / 600 ml vegetable broth (stock)

1 small chili, finely diced

Salt & freshly milled pepper

Chili powder

Sugar

1½ tbsp butter

3 tbsp flour

Scant ½ cup / 100 g whipping cream

2 oz / 50 g bacon, thinly sliced

Parsley, to garnish

Method

Prep and cook time: 30 min

1. Drain the corn kernels. Put about ¾ of the can into a small pan and add the onion, broth (stock), ¾ of the chili and seasonings and simmer, stirring occasionally, for 10–15 minutes.

2. Blend together the butter and flour to make a paste and stir it into the broth. Briefly bring the soup to a boil.

3. Finely purée the soup, adding the cream at the same time (push through a sieve if you wish). Add the rest of the sweetcorn into the soup.

4. Fry the diced bacon in a dry skillet until crisp.

5. Reheat the soup and serve sprinkled with the bacon, parsley and the rest of the chili.

Vegetable Soup
with Barley and Pork

Ingredients

½ cup /100 g barley

1 onion

2 oz / 50 g streaky bacon, diced

Salt and freshly milled pepper

Pinch nutmeg

3 cups / 700 ml beef broth (stock)

7 oz / 200 g smoked cured pork, without the bone, pre-cooked

8 oz / 250 g pumpkin

1 leek

2 stalks celery

A few celery leaves, to garnish

Method

Prep and cook time: 1 hour

1. Wash the barley and drain well. Peel and finely chop the onion. Dice the bacon and fry in a skillet, without fat. Add the barley and the onions and sauté. Season with salt, pepper and nutmeg and pour in the beef broth (stock). Bring to a boil, and then simmer for 20–25 minutes.

2. In the meantime, cut the pork into 1-inch (2–3 cm) cubes. Dice the pumpkin, wash the leek and cut into thin rings, wash the celery and cut into slices. Put the pork and the vegetables in the soup and cook until soft.

3. Season the soup to taste, garnish with a few celery leaves and serve.

Minestrone

Ingredients

4 tomatoes

Olive oil

2 onions, finely chopped

2 carrots, finely diced

2 small zucchini (courgettes), finely diced

2 garlic cloves, peeled and crushed

250 g / 2 cups passata (sieved tomatoes)

750 ml / 2½ cups vegetable broth (stock)

600 g / 3 cups canned butter beans

Basil leaves, chopped

Freshly grated Parmesan cheese

Salt and freshly milled pepper

Wholewheat bread, to serve

Method

Prep and cook time: 35 min

1. Drop the tomatoes into boiling water for a few seconds, then skin, halve, deseed and finely dice.

2. Heat 2 tbsp oil in a pan and sweat the onions, carrots, zucchini (courgettes) and garlic over a low heat for 2–3 minutes, stirring.

3. Add the passata. Cook over a very low heat until reduced slightly, then add the broth (stock).

4. Bring to a boil, stir in the diced tomato and simmer over a low heat for about 10 minutes.

5. Stir in the drained beans and basil leaves and cook gently for a further 1 minute.

6. Season to taste with salt and pepper. Sprinkle with Parmesan cheese and serve with hearty wholewheat bread.

Lentil Soup
with Ham

Ingredients

1¼ cups / 250 g lentils

1 tbsp vegetable oil

⅓ cup / 50 g diced ham

About ½ pound / 250 g celery root (celeriac), peeled and finely diced

2 carrots, peeled and finely diced

1 onion, finely diced

2 bay leaves

1 small baking potato (about 4 oz / 100 g), peeled and diced

2 tbsp butter

2 tbsp sugar

¼ cup / 50 ml light cream

Salt and freshly ground pepper, to taste

White wine vinegar, to taste

Thyme, to garnish

Method

Prep and cook time: 1 hour plus 12 hours soaking time

1. Soak the lentils overnight.

2. Heat the oil in a skillet and sauté the ham until lightly browned. Add the celery root (celeriac), carrots and onion and about 2 cups / 500 ml water. Stir in the lentils and bay leaves. Add the potato to the pan and simmer over a low heat for about 45 minutes, stirring occasionally and adding more water if necessary.

3. Melt the butter in a small skillet; add the sugar and heat, stirring, until caramelized. Stir into the lentil soup (take care—it may splatter). Remove the bay leaves. Stir in the cream, season with salt and pepper and season with vinegar. Serve, garnished with thyme.

Soybean Soup

Ingredients

7 oz / 200 g frozen soybeans

1 leek, sliced (white part only)

1 large carrot, chopped

6 scallions (spring onions) trimmed and chopped

2½ cups / 600 ml hot vegetable broth (stock)

To garnish:

1 tbsp chopped parsley

2 tbsp soft cheese, crumbled

Method

Prep and cook time: 30 min

1. Put the frozen soybeans, leek, carrot and scallions (spring onions) into a large saucepan or soup pot with the vegetable broth (stock). Bring to a boil, reduce heat and simmer for 20 minutes until the vegetables are tender.

2. Use a stick (immersion) blender to make a smooth purée (or transfer in batches to a blender or food processor).

3. Pour into bowls and serve garnished with parsley and soft cheese.

French Onion Soup
with Cheese Baguettes

Ingredients

For the soup:

2¼ lbs / 1 kg onions

2 oz / 50 g butter

4 cups / 1 liter vegetable broth (stock)

1 cup / 240 ml dry red wine

Pinch nutmeg

1 tsp fresh or ½ tsp. dried thyme

Pinch ground caraway

Salt & freshly milled pepper

For the garnish:

4–8 slices baguette

2 cloves garlic, peeled

2 oz / 50 g Gruyère cheese, grated

Bunch fresh parsley, finely chopped

Method

Prep and cook time: 45 min

1. Peel the onions and finely slice. Heat the butter in a large pan and fry the onions until soft. Pour in the vegetable broth (stock) and the wine and season with nutmeg, thyme and ground caraway. Bring to a boil, and then simmer for 25–30 minutes.

2. Toast the slices of baguette and rub a peeled garlic clove over the top of the baguette, then use a garlic press to crush the rest of the garlic into the soup.

3. Season the soup with salt and pepper and spoon into 4 ovenproof bowls. Arrange the baguette slices on top of the soup, sprinkle the grated cheese over the top and grill for a few minutes until the cheese has melted.

4. Sprinkle with finely chopped parsley and serve.

Red Lentil Soup

Ingredients

1 lb /450g pack of soup vegetables; eg carrot, leek, celery root (celeriac)

2 cups /400 g red lentils

4 cups / 1 liter beef broth (stock)

1 bay leaf

1 tsp dried thyme

2 tsp lemon zest, grated

1 tbsp tomato concentrate (purée)

3 tbsp balsamic vinegar

Salt & freshly milled pepper

Pinch sugar

For the garnish:

2 slices wholemeal bread

2 tbsp butter

Fresh basil leaves, shredded

Method

Prep and cook time: 40 min

1. Wash the soup vegetables and peel the carrot and celery root (celeriac). Finely chop. Wash the lentils in a sieve under cold, running water, then place in the beef broth (stock) and bring to a boil.

2. Add the chopped vegetables, the bay leaf and the thyme and simmer for about 20 minutes. As soon as the lentils are soft, remove the bay leaf and purée the soup.

3. Cut the crusts off the bread, cut the bread into cubes and fry in the butter until golden brown. Set aside.

4. Put the grated lemon zest and tomato concentrate (purée) in the soup, cover with a lid and warm through. Season with balsamic vinegar, salt, pepper and a pinch of sugar. Serve in warmed bowls, sprinkle a few croûtons over the top and garnish with shredded basil leaves.

Butternut Squash Soup

Ingredients

1 onion, diced

1 clove garlic, finely chopped

1 tsp ginger, finely grated

1 red chili

4 tbsp oil

1 lb 12 oz / 800 g butternut squash

1 tbsp sugar

2 cups / 500 ml vegetable broth (stock)

Scant ½ cup / 100 ml orange juice

¾–1 cup / 200 g whipping cream

Salt & freshly milled pepper

1 tsp curry powder

Ground nutmeg

Thyme, to garnish

For the croûtons:

2 slices white bread, from the previous day

2 tbsp. butter

Method

Prep and cook time: 1 hour

1. Wash the chili, slit open lengthways, remove the seeds and white inner ribs and chop finely. Peel and de-seed and dice the butternut squash.

2. Heat the oil in a pan and sauté the butternut squash, onion, garlic, ginger and chili. Sprinkle with sugar and stir over the heat until lightly caramelized. Now add the broth (stock), cover and cook gently for about 35 minutes, until soft.

3. Purée the soup. Add the orange juice and cream and bring to a boil. Season with salt and pepper and add curry powder and nutmeg to taste.

4. To make the croûtons, cut the white bread into cubes and fry in butter until golden brown. Season with salt and pepper and drain on a paper towel.

5. Ladle the hot soup into bowls and serve garnished with thyme and croûtons.

Chicken Noodle Soup

Ingredients

10 oz / 300 g chicken breast

1 tbsp rice flour, or cornstarch (cornflour)

1 clove garlic, peeled and finely chopped

½ inch / 1 cm piece ginger, peeled and finely chopped

2 tbsp sesame oil

1 tsp. curcuma (turmeric)

4 cups / 1 liter vegetable broth (stock)

1 stick lemongrass, cut into quarters lengthways

4 scallions (spring onions), cut into rings

1 small Napa cabbage (Chinese leaves), chopped

8 cherry tomatoes, quartered

2 tomatoes

7 oz / 200 g rice noodles

4 tbsp light soy sauce

4 tbsp lime juice

Thai basil, to garnish

Method
Prep and cook time: 25 min

1. Wash the chicken breasts, pat dry and cut into bite-sized pieces. Mix the chicken pieces and the rice flour in a bowl.

2. Heat the sesame oil in a saucepan and fry the chicken until lightly browned. Add the garlic, ginger, and curcuma (turmeric) and sauté, then pour in the vegetable broth (stock) and bring to a boil.

3. Add the lemongrass to the soup and simmer for about 5 minutes.

4. Put the rice noodles in the soup and simmer for a further 1–2 minutes over a low heat. Add the Napa cabbage (Chinese leaves), scallions (spring onions), cherry tomatoes and tomatoes and warm thoroughly.

5. Season to taste with soy sauce and lime juice. Garnish with Thai basil and serve.

Miso Soup
with Vegetables

Ingredients

2 tbsp miso

1 tbsp vegetable broth granules

1 small carrot, peeled and cut into matchsticks

¼ nori sheet, cut into thin strips

1 bunch radishes, trimmed and halved

½ tsp ground ginger

Salt

Method
Prep and cook time: 15 min

1. Put the miso into a pan with 3 tablespoons water and heat until it dissolves. Add 4 cups / 1 liter water and the broth granules.

2. Add the radishes, carrots and ginger to the soup and simmer for about 4 minutes. Season to taste with salt. Divide the nori strips between 4 bowls, ladle the hot soup over them and serve.

Thai Chicken Soup
with Coconut Milk

Ingredients

14 oz / about 400 g chicken breast

1 cup / 100 g oyster mushrooms

2 medium-sized tomatoes

1 red chili

1¾ cups / 400 ml coconut milk, canned, unsweetened

2¼ cups / 600 ml water

1–2 tsp ginger, freshly grated

4 tbsp fish sauce

4 tbsp lime juice

Sugar

Salt

1 tbsp freshly chopped cilantro (coriander)

Method

Prep and cook time: 35 min

1. Cut the chicken breasts into bite-size pieces. Clean the oyster mushrooms and slice. Wash, quarter, de-seed the tomatoes and chop. Wash the chili, cut in half lengthways, de-seed and finely chop.

2. Heat the coconut milk in a pan together with the water and bring to a boil.

3. Add the chicken, mushrooms, tomatoes, ginger and chili and season to taste with fish sauce and lime juice. Simmer for about 5 minutes. Add sugar and salt to taste and sprinkle chopped cilantro (coriander) over the top and serve.

Fish Soup
with Potatoes

Ingredients

2 tbsp olive oil

2 onions, finely chopped

2 cloves garlic, finely chopped

1–2 small red chilies, de-seeded and finely chopped

1 packet saffron threads

14 oz / 400 g chopped canned tomatoes

1 tbsp tomato paste (purée)

¾–1 cup / 200 ml white wine

14 oz / 400 g small whole potatoes, for boiling

Salt & freshly milled pepper

12 oz / 350 g mixed seafood, such as mussels, clams, shrimps, squid

1 lb 6 oz / 600 g fish fillets, such as cod, perch, tuna

½ bunch fresh parsley, chopped

Method

Prep and cook time: 1 hour

1. Heat the olive oil in a large skillet. Fry the onions, garlic, chili and saffron threads over a medium heat for about 10 minutes.

2. Add the tomatoes, tomato paste (purée) and pour in the white wine. Bring to a boil, then reduce the heat and simmer for 5 minutes.

3. Peel the potatoes and dice if necessary, and then add to the pan and simmer gently for 15 minutes. Season with salt and pepper.

4. Wash and clean the seafood and add to the soup. Place the fish fillets on the top. Cover and simmer for a further 10 minutes over a medium heat.

5. Spoon into 4 bowls, sprinkle with freshly chopped parsley and serve.

Split Pea Soup

Ingredients

1 lb / 450 g dried green split peas, rinsed

6 oz / 175 g bacon, diced

3 carrots, sliced

1 onion, chopped

1 garlic clove, finely chopped

1 bay leaf

Salt, to taste

½ tsp pepper

6 cups / 1.5 liters hot water

4 slices of bacon, diced, to garnish

Method

Prep and cook time: 1 hour plus 12 hours soaking

1. Soak the split peas for 12 hours in cold water.

2. Rinse and put in a large pan. Cover with the water. Bring to a boil and simmer for 25 minutes.

3. Skim off any scum and add the bacon, vegetables, garlic and the bay leaf. Season with salt and pepper. Simmer for 15–20 minutes, until the peas are tender.

4. Cool slightly, then mash with a potato masher to make a thick soup.

5. Fry the bacon until just crisp and stir into the soup.

Classic Vinaigrette

Ingredients

1 small shallot, very finely chopped

1 tbsp white wine vinegar

¾ tsp Dijon mustard

Plenty of freshly ground black pepper

6 tbs extra virgin olive oil

Sprinkle of sea salt (optional)

Method

Put all the ingredients in a jar and shake until well emulsified.

For a milder version

- Omit the mustard or use less
- Use white pepper instead of black pepper
- Use vegetable oil or a milder tasting olive oil

For an Asian feel

- Substitute ½ tsp of olive oil for sesame or chili oil
- Substitute rice vinegar for white wine vinegar

Orange version – perfect with spinach salads

- Add 1 tbsp runny honey
- Add the juice and zest of 1 large orange
- Use balsamic instead of white wine vinegar

Chili and Coriander Vinaigrette

Ingredients

1 red chili pepper

1 green chili pepper

½ cup / 10 g cilantro (fresh coriander) leaves

½ cup / 10 g fresh Thai basil

2 garlic cloves, peeled

8 tsp rice vinegar

2 tbsp soy sauce

⅓ cup / 75 ml vegetable oil

Salt

Method

Prep and cook time: 10 min

1. Rinse and slice the chilis in half. lengthwise. Remove the ribs and seeds.

2. Put the chilis, cilantro (coriander), basil, garlic cloves, vinegar, soy sauce and half of the oil in a food processor and make a fine purée.

3. Mix in the remaining oil and season with salt to taste.

Tomato and Oregano Vinaigrette

Ingredients

¾ cup / 150 g canned tomatoes, finely chopped

4 tbsp white wine vinegar

1 tsp honey

6 tbsp olive oil

4 sprigs oregano

Salt

Cayenne pepper

Method

Prep and cook time: 10 min

1. Mix together the tomatoes, vinegar, honey, 2–3 tbsp of water and the olive oil.

2. Remove the oregano leaves from the stems. Reserve a few for garnishing. Finely chop the rest and mix in with the vinaigrette.

3. Season to taste with salt and cayenne pepper.

4. Garnish with the reserved oregano leaves.

Garlic Mayonnaise

Ingredients

5 large garlic cloves

3 egg yolks

1 tsp hot mustard

Salt

White pepper

1⅓ cups / 300 ml olive oil

½ tbsp lemon juice

Method

Prep and cook time: 15 min

1. Peel and crush the garlic cloves.

2. Combine the egg yolks, garlic, mustard and a pinch of salt and pepper in a large bowl. Beat until creamy.

3. Add the oil, drop by drop beating constantly. Incorporate the oil completely into the mixture before adding more. As the mixture thickens you can begin to add the oil in a slow, steady stream. When the oil is fully incorporated, stir in the lemon juice.

4. Season with salt and pepper to taste and serve.

Béchamel Sauce

Ingredients

1 shallot

2 tbsp butter

2 tbsp flour

Generous ¾ cup / 200 ml beef broth (stock)

Generous ¾ cup / 200 ml milk

1 bay leaf

Nutmeg

3 tbsp whipping cream

1 tsp lemon juice

Salt and freshly ground pepper

Method

Prep and cook time: 20 min

1. Peel and finely dice the shallot.

2. Heat the butter in a saucepan until foamy. Add the shallot and sauté until translucent.

3. Stir in the flour. Continue to stir and sauté until the flour begins to lighten.

4. Gradually whisk in the broth (stock) and the milk. Add the bay leaf. Season with nutmeg, salt and pepper.

5. Bring the sauce to a boil while stirring. Simmer, stirring occasionally, for about 15 minutes over low heat.

6. Add the cream and lemon juice to taste and season with salt and pepper.

Cocktail Sauce

Ingredients

²/₃ cup / 150 g mayonnaise

3 tbsp ketchup

1 tsp horseradish sauce

Lemon juice

Worcestershire sauce

Salt

Cayenne pepper

1 tbsp chives, to garnish

Method

Prep and cook time: 10 min

1. Mix together the mayonnaise, ketchup and horseradish sauce until smooth.

2. Season to taste with the lemon juice, Worcestershire sauce and cayenne pepper.

3. Garnish with the chives and serve as a dip with shrimps.

Hollandaise Sauce

Ingredients

8 oz / 2 sticks / 250 g butter

1 tbsp white wine vinegar

½ cup / 125 ml dry white wine

3 egg yolks

Lemon juice

Salt

Method

Prep and cook time: 30 min

1. Melt the butter over medium heat.

2. Put the vinegar and wine in a small saucepan and heat until the volume of liquid is reduced by half. Allow to cool.

3. Put the egg yolks in a metal bowl and add the reduced liquid. Place the bowl over a pan of gently simmering water and whisk the eggs and liquid until creamy.

4. Add the butter drop by drop as the sauce emulsifies and then in a stream.

5. Season to taste with the lemon juice and salt.

Pepper Sauce with Cream

Ingredients

1 onion

2 tbsp butter

1 tbsp black pepper corns

2 tbsp flour

Generous ¾ cup / 200 ml beef broth (stock)

7 tbsp / 100 ml whipping cream

2 tbsp green pepper corns, from a jar

Salt and freshly ground pepper

1 tbsp crème frâiche, to serve

Method

Prep and cook time: 20 min

1. Peel and finely chop the onion. Sauté in hot butter until translucent.

2. Add the coarsely crushed black pepper corns and sauté briefly.

3. Sprinkle in the flour and stir in the beef broth (stock).

4. Add the cream and simmer for approximately 10 minutes, stirring occasionally.

5. To finish stir in the green pepper corns and season with salt. Serve garnished with a swirl of crème frâiche and some freshly ground pepper.

Citrus Dressing

Ingredients

1 lime

1 orange

¼ cup / 50 ml sour cream

²/₃ cup / 150 g yogurt

About 1 tsp brown sugar

Salt

Mint leaves, for garnishing

Method

Prep and cook time: 15 min

1. Remove the zest from the lime and the orange. Blanch briefly in hot water. Refresh and drain.

2. Squeeze the juice from the fruit.

3. Stir the juice, ²/₃ of the zest, the sour cream, yogurt and sugar (to taste) until smooth. Season to taste with salt and put into a bowl.

4. Garnish with the reserved zest and mint.

Parmesan Sauce

Ingredients

²/₃ cup / 150 ml hot vegetable
broth (stock)

3 tbsp white wine vinegar

4 tbsp olive oil

1 cup / 100 g freshly grated
Parmesan cheese

Method

Prep and cook time: 5 min

1. Mix together the vegetable broth (stock), vinegar, oil and
Parmesan cheese in a pan. Heat gently for a few minutes.

2. Season to taste with salt and pepper.

Bread Sauce

Ingredients

1 onion

2 cloves

1 fresh bay leaf

1²/₃ cups / 400 ml milk

4 oz / 100 g white bread, crusts removed

2 tbsp butter

2 tbsp crème frâiche

Salt and freshly ground pepper

Nutmeg

2 fresh bay leaves, for garnishing

Method

Prep and cook time: 40 min

1. Peel the onion and stud it with the cloves.

2. Put the onion, milk and bay leaf in a saucepan and bring to a
boil. Simmer very gently for approximately 15 minutes.

3. Remove the onion and the bay leaf.

4. Crumble the bread into the milk. Remove from the heat and
allow to soak for 15 minutes.

5. Stir in the butter and crème frâiche. Add salt, pepper and
nutmeg to taste.

6. Fill a bowl with the sauce. Serve sprinkled with nutmeg and
garnished with the bay leaves.

Cranberry and Pistachio Sauce

Ingredients

2 onions

3 cups / 300 g cranberries

2 tbsp vegetable oil

²/₃ cup / 150 ml red wine

1 cup / 200 g canned tomatoes, chopped

²/₃ cup / 100 g pistachio nuts

Brown sugar

Salt

Cayenne pepper

Method

Prep and cook time: 40 min

1. Peel and coarsely chop the onions.

2. Rinse and drain the cranberries.

3. Sauté the onions in a little hot oil.

4. Mix in the cranberries and tomatoes in a pan and pour in the
red wine. Coarsely chop the pistachios and add them to mixture.

5. Simmer the sauce, stirring occasionally, for about 30 minutes.

6. Season to taste with the sugar, salt and cayenne pepper.

Lemon Barbecue Sauce

Ingredients

2 garlic cloves

4 tbsp lemon juice

¼ cup / 50 ml dry white wine

4 tbsp vegetable oil

2 sprigs thyme

1 tsp fennel seed

Method

Prep and cook time: 5 min

1. Peel and slice the garlic.

2. Mix together the garlic, lemon juice, oil, thyme and fennel. Use to marinate and baste steaks or pork.

Herb and Chili Marinade

Ingredients

3 garlic cloves

1 shallot

2 cups / 40 g chopped fresh herbs, rosemary, mint, basil

1 red chili pepper, deseeded and finely chopped

¼ cup / 50 ml olive oil

1 tsp hot mustard

2 tbsp white balsamic vinegar

Method

Prep and cook time: 10 min

1. Peel and finely chop the garlic cloves and shallot.

2. Combine the garlic, shallots, chili pepper and herbs in a bowl.

3. Stir the olive oil, mustard, pepper and balsamic vinegar into the herbs. Season with salt and pepper to taste.

Barbecue Marinade

Ingredients

1 red chili pepper

6 tbsp soy sauce

2 tbsp liquid honey

4 tbsp mild sesame oil

2 tsp finely chopped ginger

1 tsp finely chopped lemon grass

Method

Prep and cook time: 5 min

1. Deseed the chili pepper and slice into rings. Mix together with the soy sauce, honey, oil, ginger and lemon grass.

2. Use to marinate and baste barbecue meats

Thai Soy Dip

Ingredients

4 scallions (spring onions)

2 garlic cloves

2 red chili peppers

1 tsp fresh ginger, peeled and grated

1¼ cups / 300 ml soy sauce

2 tbsp sesame oil

1 tbsp honey

Method

Prep and cook time: 10 min

1. Remove the roots and ragged tops from the scallions (spring onions). Rinse and slice into long, very narrow strips.

2. Peel and finely chop the garlic cloves.

3. Rinse the chili peppers and slice them in half. Remove the seeds and ribs and slice into strips.

4. Mix together the peppers, scallions, garlic, ginger, soy sauce, oil and honey.

Basil and Pine Nut (Classic) Pesto

Ingredients

½ cup / 50 g pine nuts

½ cup / 50 g Parmesan cheese

3 cups / 60 g fresh basil

2 garlic cloves, peeled

About 7 tbsp / 100 ml olive oil

Salt and freshly ground pepper

Method

Prep and cook time: 15 min

1. Toast the pine nuts in a dry pan until lightly browned.

2. Finely grate the Parmesan cheese.

3. Remove the basil leaves from the stems. Rinse and pat dry.

4. Put the pine nuts, basil and garlic in a food processor. Add half the oil and finely purée.

5. Add the cheese and purée briefly.

6. Mix in enough of the remaining oil to make a creamy pesto. Season with salt and pepper to taste.

7. Pour into a jar and cover with a thin layer of olive oil. Close well. The sauce will keep for at least 3 days if refrigerated.

Tomato Salsa

Ingredients

6 tomatoes

1 red onion

2 scallions (spring onions), green parts only

3 tbsp olive oil

Salt

Sugar

Lemon juice

Cayenne pepper

Method

Prep and cook time: 15 min

1. Rinse, quarter and remove the seeds from the tomato and dice the flesh.

2. Peel and chop the onion. Rinse and slice the scallion (spring onion) greens diagonally into thin rings.

3. Mix the tomatoes, onion, green scallions and olive oil together.

4. Season to taste with salt, sugar, lemon juice and cayenne pepper. Serve with corn chips.

Green Melon Salsa

Ingredients

1 Galia melon

1 lime

1 jalepeno pepper, deseeded and sliced into rings

1 red chili pepper, deseeded and finely chopped

$^2/_3$ cup /150 ml water

2 tbsp sugar

1 tbsp fresh, chopped basil

Method

Prep and cook time: 15 min

1. Slice the melon in half. Remove the seeds, peel and finely dice.

2. Remove the zest from the lime and squeeze out the juice. Put the lime juice, zest, sugar and the water in a saucepan. Bring to a boil and simmer for 4–5 minutes.

3. Add the jalepeno and chili peppers and the basil.

4. Pour the sauce over the diced melon. Mix well and allow to cool.

Sweet and Sour Chili Sauce

Ingredients

4 red chili peppers

2 garlic cloves

1 cup / 250 ml water

¼ cup / 50 ml mild white wine vinegar

2 tbsp honey

Lemon juice

Method

Prep and cook time: 50 min

1. Rinse the chili peppers. Remove the ribs and stem and finely chop.

2. Peel and finely chop the garlic cloves.

3. Combine the chilis, garlic and vinegar with the water and bring to a boil. Simmer over low heat for about 40 minutes until the sauce thickens.

4. Season to taste with honey and lemon juice.

Green Mojo Sauce

Ingredients

1 cup / 20 g cilantro (fresh coriander) leaves

1 cup / 20 g fresh parsley

1 shallot, peeled

2 garlic cloves, peeled

About $^1/_3$ cup / 80 ml olive oil

Lemon juice

Salt and freshly ground black pepper

Method

Prep and cook time: 15 min

1. Remove the cilantro (coriander) and parsley leaves from the stems. Rinse and shake off any excess water.

2. Finely purée the herbs, shallot and garlic cloves with the olive oil in a food processor.

3. Season to taste with salt and pepper.

4. Use as a dip for white crusty bread.

Sour Cream Dip

Ingredients

2 garlic cloves

1 1/3 cups / 300 ml sour cream

Salt and freshly ground black pepper

2 tbsp oilve oil

Chives, for garnishing

Method

Prep and cook time: 10 min

1. Peel and finely chop the garlic cloves. Add a pinch of salt.

2. Using the flat side of a knife, crush the garlic into a paste.

3. Mix the garlic paste into the sour cream. Stir until smooth. Season to taste with salt and the pepper.

4. Fill small bowls with the sour cream. Sprinkle with pepper and drizzle a little oil over the top. Garnish with chives and serve.

Avocado Dip

Ingredients

1 shallot

2 ripe avocados

1 lime

1 tbsp fresh, chopped cilantro (coriander)

Salt and freshly ground black pepper

Cayenne pepper

1 tbsp chives, for garnishing

Method

Prep and cook time: 15 min

1. Peel and finely chop the shallot.

2. Slice the avocados in half. Remove the pit and scoop out the flesh.

3. Cut the lime in half and squeeze out the juice.

4. Purée the avocados with the juice and cilantro (coriander) until smooth.

5. Stir in the shallot. Season to taste with salt, pepper and cayenne pepper. Garnish with the chives and a little cayenne pepper.

White Bean Purée

Ingredients

1 1/4 cup / 250 g dried lima (haricot) beans, soaked overnight

1 onion

2 garlic cloves

4 tbsp olive oil

2 cups / 500 ml chicken broth (stock)

4 sprigs thyme

2 tbsp crème fraîche

Salt and freshly ground black pepper

Method

Prep and cook time: 1 hour plus 12 hours soaking time

1. Peel and finely chop the onon and garlic.

2. Heat 1 tbsp olive oil in a large pan and cook the onion and garlic until translucent.

3. Add the broth (stock) with the drained beans and 3 thyme sprigs. Cook until the beans are soft, stirring occasionally (about 45 minutes).

4. Drain the beans, reserving the cooking broth.

5. Remove the thyme sprigs from the beans and purée the mixture until smooth.

6. Stir in the crème fraîche, 2 tbsp of oil and enough broth to form a creamy purée.

7. Season with salt and pepper to taste. Drizzle the remaining olive oil over the top. Remove the leaves from the remaining thyme sprig and use as garnish.

Pepper Dip

Ingredients

3 red bell peppers

1 red chili pepper, deseeded and chopped

1 clove garlic, peeled and roughly chopped

1 cup / 250 g full fat cream cheese

2 tbsp mayonnaise

2 tbsp olive oil

¼ tsp paprika, for garnishing

Rosemary leaves, for garnishing

Red chili pepper, for garnishing

Method

Prep and cook time: 30 min

1. Place the bell peppers under a hot broiler (grill) and broil until the skins start to blacken and blister, turning from time to time. Let cool.

2. Carefully remove the blackened skins and scrape out the seeds.

3. Put the peppers and all the other ingredients into a food processor and blend until smooth; add a little water if the mix is too stiff.

4. Season with salt and pepper and garnish with a few slices of chili pepper, rosemary leaves and a pinch of paprika.

STARTERS
AND SNACKS

Tomatoes
Stuffed with Cheese and Herbs

Ingredients

4 large tomatoes

Salt & freshly milled pepper

3 tbsp olive oil

1 slice white bread, diced

1 tsp chopped rosemary

1 tsp chopped parsley

5–7 oz / 150–200 g sheep's cheese

Method

Prep and cook time: 40 min

1. Preheat the oven to 400°F (200°C / Gas Mark 6). Wash the tomatoes and cut a lid from each one. Hollow out the tomatoes and season inside with salt. Turn over and stand on paper towel to draw out some of the water.

2. Heat 2 tablespoons oil and fry the diced bread. Add the herbs, season with salt and pepper and leave to cool. Then mix with the crumbled sheep's cheese.

3. Fill the tomatoes with the stuffing and put into a baking dish greased with 1 teaspoon oil. Put the lids on the tomatoes.

4. Sprinkle with the remaining oil and bake for about 25 minutes.

Grilled Vegetables

Ingredients

2 zucchinis (courgettes)

2 eggplants (aubergines)

2 red bell peppers

2 white onions

2 tomatoes

2 garlic cloves

6 tbsp olive oil

1 sprig rosemary, chopped

Lemon wedges, for garnishing

Method

Prep and cook time: 20 min

1. Rinse the zucchinis (courgettes) and eggplants (aubergines). Remove the tops/stems. Slice lengthwise into ¼ inch / ½ cm thick slices.

2. Salt the eggplant slices. Soak them in water for about 10 minutes.

3. Slice the bell peppers in half. Remove the ribs and seeds. Slice in half again.

4. Peel the onions and slice into wedges.

5. Rinse the tomatoes and cut out the stems. Slice in half.

6. Peel and finely chop the garlic and combine with the olive oil.

7. Pat the eggplant slices dry. Brush all the vegetables with oil.

8. Heat a ridged skillet or griddle pan and cook the vegetables in batches, turning frequently and brushing occasionally with the oil, until they are tender.

9. Arrange the vegetables on a platter. Remove the skin from the peppers if desired. Season with salt and pepper. Sprinkle with the rosemary and garnish with lemon wedges.

Potato, Bean and Avocado Salad

Ingredients

1 lb 6 oz / 600 g salad potatoes

1 lb / 500 g green and yellow beans

4 oz / 100 g bacon, sliced

1 tbsp oil

2 tbsp yogurt

1 tbsp crème fraîche

Juice of 1 lemon

1 pinch sugar

Salt & freshly milled pepper

2 avocados

Dill weed tips, to garnish

Method

Prep and cook time: 40 min

1. Wash the potatoes and steam for about 20 minutes, or until cooked. Leave to cool until lukewarm then halve each potato.

2. Wash and trim the beans and blanch in boiling, salted water for 3–4 minutes until al dente. Refresh in cold water and drain well.

3. Cut the bacon into strips. Heat the oil and fry the bacon until golden brown, then drain on paper towel.

4. Mix the yogurt and crème fraîche smoothly with the lemon juice. Add sugar and salt to taste.

5. Peel and halve the avocados, remove the pits and cut the fruit into wedges. Arrange on 4 plates at once with the other ingredients and sprinkle with the dressing. Season with freshly milled pepper and serve garnished with dill tips.

Halloumi and Anchovy Salad

Ingredients

1 lb / 600 g green beans, trimmed

5–6 mild red chili peppers

8–10 oil-packed anchovies, drained

1 head radicchio lettuce, leaves separated

10–12 sage leaves

Juice of 1 lemon

4–5 tbsp olive oil

Salt and freshly ground pepper, to taste

14 oz / 400 g halloumi cheese, sliced*

Method

Prep and cook time: 30 min

1. Bring a large saucepan of salted water to boil. Add the beans and cook until tender-crisp, 8–10 minutes. Drain in a colander under cold running water to stop the cooking; set aside.

2. Meanwhile, preheat the broiler (grill). Wearing gloves to prevent irritation, slice chilies in half lengthwise and remove the seeds; slice into strips. Pat the anchovies dry with a paper towel.

3. Combine the beans, radicchio, chilies, anchovies and sage; drizzle with the lemon juice and olive oil. Season with salt and pepper.

4. Broil (grill) the cheese until golden brown on both sides. Arrange the salad onto plates, place a few slices of cheese on the top and serve.

*Halloumi (or haloumi), from Cyprus, is a semi-soft cheese usually made from goat's and sheep milk; its firm texture makes it suitable for frying or grilling. If unavailable substitute firm mozzarella or feta.

Baba Ghanoush with Pita

Ingredients

2¼ lb / 1 kg eggplants (aubergines)

1 small onion, coarsely chopped

2 tsp chopped fresh parsley

3–4 cloves garlic, chopped

About ½ cup / 100 g olive oil

3–6 tablespoons lemon juice

Salt and white pepper, to taste

4 pita breads

Method

Prep and cook time: 45 min

1. Preheat the grill (or preheat the oven to 400°F (200°C /Gas Mark 6). Pierce the eggplants (aubergines) in several places with a fork. Grill or bake until the skin blisters and wrinkles and the flesh is soft. Let cool, then halve lengthwise and scrape out the flesh, discarding the skin.

2. Roughly chop the eggplant flesh and purée in a blender or food processor with the onion, parsley and garlic. Stir in enough olive oil to produce a creamy paste. Season with salt and pepper and add lemon juice to taste. Spoon into four small bowls, cover and chill.

3. Warm the pita breads according to the package instructions: heat them in the oven or toast briefly on both sides in a dry skillet (frying pan). Slice into strips and serve with the eggplant purée.

Smoked Mackerel and Horseradish Pâté

Ingredients

450 g / 1 lb smoked mackerel

225 g / 1 cup crème fraîche

2 tbsp ready-made creamed horseradish

400 g / 2 cups beet (beetroot), peeled and finely chopped

2 shallots, peeled and finely chopped

1 apple, peeled, cored and finely chopped

4 tbsp brown sugar

4 tbsp red wine vinegar

2 tbsp lemon juice

About 3 tbsp red wine (optional)

2 tbsp parsley, chopped

Salt

Method

Prep and cook time: 30 min plus 2½ hours to chill and marinate

1. In a food processor, blend the mackerel, crème fraîche and creamed horseradish to a smooth consistency. Season with pepper, spoon into four small dishes and chill for at least 2 hours.

2. Mix together the chopped beets (beetroot), shallots and apple.

3. Add the sugar, vinegar and lemon juice and marinate for about 20 minutes.

4. Bring to a boil and simmer for 15–20 minutes, stirring occasionally, until cooked.

5. If necessary, add a little red wine but do not let the relish become too liquid.

6. Season with salt, add parsley and let cool. Serve the pâté and relish with whole-grain bread if desired.

Crab Salad Boats

Ingredients

8 oz / about 200 g cooked crab meat,
picked over to remove shells

1 shallot, finely chopped

2 tbsp mayonnaise

1 tbsp sour cream

Salt and cayenne pepper, to taste

12 large Belgian endive leaves

2 oz / 50 g pistachios, roughly chopped

2 plums, pitted and sliced into
thin strips

Method

Prep and cook time: 20 min

1. Mix together the crab meat, shallot, mayonnaise, and sour cream in a bowl. Season with salt and cayenne pepper.

2. Place a spoonful of crab salad onto each endive leaf. Sprinkle each with chopped pistachios, then scatter a few slices of plum on top. Serve immediately.

Bruschetta with Tomatoes and Basil

Ingredients

2 garlic cloves

3 beef tomatoes

2 sprigs basil

Lemon juice, to taste

8 thin slices baguette

2–3 tbsp olive oil

Salt and freshly ground pepper

Method

Prep and cook time: 20 min

1. Preheat the oven to 475°F (240°C / Gas Mark 9).

2. Peel the garlic. Slice the cloves in half.

3. Quarter the tomatoes. Remove the seeds and chop.

4. Remove the basil leaves from the stem. Set a few aside for garnishing. Coarsely chop the rest.

5. Mix the basil leaves with the tomatoes and lemon juice. Season with salt and pepper to taste.

6. Toast the bread slices in the oven (lay directly on a rack) for about 2 minutes, until golden brown.

7. Rub the hot slices with the garlic and drizzle with olive oil. Place some tomatoes on top of each slice. Garnish with the reserved basil leaves and serve.

Tomato and Bread Skewers on Parma Ham

Ingredients

3–4 thick slices white bread, cut into 1-inch (3-cm) cubes

2 cloves garlic

About ¼ cup / 50 ml olive oil

16 cherry tomatoes

2 sprigs thyme, leaves

6–8 small gherkins

8 slices Parma ham

2 tbsp extra virgin olive oil

1 tbsp lemon juice

Salt & coarsely milled pepper

Wooden skewers

Method

Prep and cook time: 15 min

1. Purée the garlic finely with the oil and briefly toss the bread cubes in the flavored oil. Preheat the broiler (grill).

2. Wash and dry the tomatoes and thread on wooden skewers with the bread, alternating tomatoes with bread. Sprinkle with thyme.

3. Cook on all sides under a hot broiler (grill) for about 5 minutes.

4. Drain the gherkins, slice lengthways and put on plates with the Parma ham. Mix the oil with the lemon juice and sprinkle over the gherkins and ham. Arrange the skewers on top and season lightly with pepper and salt. Serve at once.

Bread Salad with Tomatoes

Ingredients

1 ciabatta loaf, day-old

8 tbsp olive oil

8 tomatoes

1 cup / 20 g fresh basil leaves

½ cup / 50 g black olives, pitted

2 red onions

1 garlic clove

½ cucumber

2 tbsp white balsamic vinegar

2 tbsp lemon juice

Salt and freshly ground pepper

Method

Prep and cook time: 30 min

1. Cut the ciabatta into cubes. Sauté in 3 tbsp of olive oil until golden brown and crispy. Drain the croûtons on paper towel.

2. Rinse the tomatoes, remove the stems and slice into wedges.

3. Remove the basil leaves from the stems. Coarsely chop.

4. Slice the olives in half.

5. Peel the onion and cut in half. Slice into strips.

6. Peel and finely chop the garlic.

7. Peel the cucumber and cut in half lengthwise. Remove the seeds and slice.

8. Put the tomatoes, olives, onion, cucumber and garlic in a dish. Mix with the remaining oil, balsamic vinegar and lemon juice. Season to taste with salt and pepper. Allow to marinate for 10 minutes.

9. Mix in the basil and croûtons. Season to taste again and serve.

Bean and Tomato Crostini

Ingredients

7 oz / 200 g canned white beans

1 small red onion, quartered and cut into short, thin strips

2 cloves garlic

1–2 tbsp balsamic vinegar

1–2 tbsp lemon juice

Salt & freshly milled black pepper

3–4 tbsp extra virgin olive oil

2 tsp lemon zest

4 small bunches tomatoes on the vine

1½ cups / 25–50 g arugula (rocket)

8 slices rustic Italian white bread, or ciabatta

Method

Prep and cook time: 20 min

1. Rinse and drain the beans. Peel the garlic and finely chop 1 clove. Halve the other.

2. Mix the balsamic vinegar with the chopped garlic, lemon juice, salt, pepper, and olive oil, then mix with the lemon zest, onion, and beans.

3. Put the bread and the tomatoes into a hot oven (400°F / 200°C / Gas Mark 6) until the bread is toasted and the tomatoes are cooked. Rub the bread with the halved garlic clove. Pile spoonfuls of the vegetable mixture on each slice and top with arugula (rocket) and tomatoes. Serve at once.

Green Beans with Parma Ham

Ingredients

Makes 8 bundles

1 lb 12 oz / 800 g green beans

8 large slices Parma ham

8 thick chives

For the sauce:

8 oz / 2 sticks / 250 g butter

2 egg yolks

4 tbsp dry white wine

2 tbsp lemon juice

Salt & freshly milled white pepper

Method

Prep and cook time: 30 min

1. Wash and trim the beans and blanch in boiling, salted water for 6–8 minutes, until al dente. Drain in a colander under cold running water to stop the cooking; set aside.

2. Meanwhile make the sauce: clarify the butter by melting it and skimming off the foam. Put the egg yolks and wine into a metal bowl and beat over a pan of simmering water until foamy. Then add the butter, in drops at first, then in a thin stream, beating constantly until you have a creamy, homogenous sauce. The egg yolks must not curdle – don't let it boil! Season with salt and pepper and add lemon juice to taste.

3. Divide the beans into 8 portions, carefully wrap a slice of Parma ham around each bundle and tie with a chive. Serve on warmed plates, pour a little sauce over the bundles and hand the rest of the sauce separately.

Stuffed Eggplant Slices

Ingredients

1–2 eggplants (aubergine)sliced
lengthwise ½-¾ inch / 1-2 cm thick

Salt, as needed

About 8 oz / 200 g fresh goat cheese

1–2 tbsp chopped fresh herbs of
your choice

Salt and freshly ground pepper, to taste

2–3 tbsp olive oil

Lemon juice, for sprinkling

Method

Prep and cook time: 25 min

1. Sprinkle the eggplant (aubergine) slices on both sides with salt.
Cover and let stand for at least 10 minutes to draw out some of
the water, then rinse and pat the individual slices dry.

2. Meanwhile, mix the goat cheese with the herbs and season
with salt and pepper.

3. Heat the oil in a nonstick skillet (frying pan) and quickly sauté
the eggplant slices on both sides. Remove from the skillet and
sprinkle with lemon juice. Then season with pepper, spread with
the herbed cheese and roll up. Serve lukewarm.

Artichokes with Mustard Dressing

Ingredients

4 artichokes

Juice of ½ lemon

For the vinaigrette:

6 tbsp olive oil

2 tbsp white wine vinegar

2 tsp Dijon mustard

1 clove garlic

Sea salt & freshly milled white pepper

Method

Prep and cook time: 40 min

1. Wash the artichokes. Stand the artichokes side by side in a wide pan, half fill with water and add the lemon juice. Put a lid on the pan and cook over a medium heat for 25–30 minutes, until the leaves pull away easily.

2. Peel and finely chop the garlic and crush with 2 pinches of sea salt. Mix with the vinegar, mustard and pepper and whisk in the oil. Season to taste.

3. Drain the artichokes well and serve on plates with a small dish of vinaigrette.

Mussels au Gratin

Ingredients

2¼ lb / 1 kg fresh mussels

1 cup / 20 g fresh parsley, chopped

8 tbsp olive oil

2 cups / 200 g bread crumbs

½ red chili, deseeded and chopped

1 tbsp freshly grated Parmesan cheese

1 garlic clove, chopped

Salt and freshly ground pepper

Method

Prep and cook time: 25 min

1. Preheat the oven to 400°F (200°C / Gas Mark 6).

2. Scrub the mussels well with a small metal brush and wash under running water. Put into a large pan and cover with water, put a lid on the pan and bring to a boil over a high heat.

3. Cook until the mussels open (throw away any that do not open). Drain (reserve 1 cup / 250 ml of the cooking water), then remove the empty halves of the shells and place the halves containing the mussels on a baking tray.

4. Wash the parsley, shake dry and chop finely. Heat 3 tbsp olive oil in a skillet (frying pan) and fry the bread crumbs, stirring, until golden brown.

5. Mix together the parsley, chili, bread crumbs, Parmesan cheese, garlic, 5 tbsp oil and 1–2 tbsp of the mussel water. Season with salt and pepper.

6. Place a little of the mixture on top of each mussel and press down slightly. Put the baking tray into the preheated oven for about 2 minutes, until the gratin topping is nicely browned.

Shrimp Cakes
with Sweet-and-Sour Sauce

Ingredients

1¾ lb / 800 g shrimp (prawns), peeled, de-veined, and finely chopped

1 small hot chili pepper

3 cloves garlic, chopped

2 sprigs cilantro (fresh coriander), leaves separated

½ tsp salt

Freshly ground pepper, to taste

1 egg

2 cups / 500 ml neutral-tasting vegetable oil, such as canola or grapeseed

Sweet-and-sour sauce, for dipping

Method

Prep and cook time: 20 min

1. Finely chop the shrimp (prawns). Wearing gloves to prevent irritation, seed and de-vein the chili and finely chop. Crush the garlic, chili and cilantro (coriander) leaves in a mortar with the salt and pepper. Add the shrimp and blend to a paste. Add the egg and mix well.

2. Form the mixture into approximately 2-inch (5-cm) patties, using 2 tablespoons of the mixture for each one.

3. In a large skillet (frying pan), heat the oil and fry the shrimp cakes for about 2 minutes, until golden brown. Drain on paper towels. Serve at once with the sweet-and-sour sauce.

Onion Bhajis

Ingredients

2 onions

2 green chilies

½ tsp chili powder

2 tbsp finely chopped cilantro (coriander) leaves

3 tbsp lemon juice

1 tsp cumin seeds, roughly crushed in a mortar

7 tbsp chickpea flour (gram flour)

Pinch of salt

2 tbsp water

2 cups / 500 ml sunflower oil, for deep-frying

Method

Prep and cook time: 40 min

1. Peel the onions and slice into very thin rings. Wash the chilies, slit open lengthways, remove the seeds and white inner ribs and finely dice the flesh. Mix both with the chili powder, cilantro (coriander), lemon juice and cumin.

2. Stir the chickpea flour and salt into the onion mixture. Add the water and mix well.

3. Heat the oil in a pan (it is hot enough when bubbles form on the handle of a wooden spoon held in the oil). Take small balls of the onion mixture with a teaspoon and fry in the hot oil, a few at a time, until golden. Drain on a paper towel and keep warm in the oven at the lowest heat. When all the bhajis are cooked, serve at once.

Chicken Satay with Coconut Sauce

Ingredients

4 chicken legs, skinned

3 tbsp oil, divided

Spice blend (¼ teaspoon each of ground ginger, cayenne pepper, black and white pepper)

2 chili peppers, de-seeded and finely chopped

3 shallots, finely chopped

2 cloves garlic, minced

1 tsp grated fresh ginger root

⅔ cup / 150 ml dry white wine

1 cup / 250 ml unsweetened coconut milk

½ cup (about 125 g) crème fraîche

1 tbsp honey

Freshly ground pepper, to taste

2 tbsp chopped cilantro (coriander leaves)

1 tbsp fish sauce, or to taste

Method

Cook and prep time: 35 min

1. Soak the wooden skewers in enough water to cover them for 20 minutes (to prevent burning).

2. Meanwhile, slice the chicken off the bone and dice. Mix 2 tablespoons of the oil with the spice blend and combine with the chicken. Preheat the broiler or grill.

3. Heat the rest of the oil in a skillet; add the shallots and garlic and sauté until softened but not browned. Stir in the ginger and chilies; add wine and cook, stirring to loosen bits from the skillet. Boil until reduced, then remove from the heat and add the coconut milk, crème fraîche, honey and ground pepper. Simmer, stirring occasionally, to produce a creamy sauce. Strain through a sieve and add the cilantro (coriander) and fish sauce to taste.

4. Shape the chicken mixture into oblongs, thread onto skewers and broil or grill for 5–6 minutes, turning frequently, until cooked through. Arrange on plates and serve with the sauce.

Frittata with Potato and Peas

Ingredients

1½ lb / 675 g waxy potatoes

1 cup / 20 g baby spinach leaves

6 eggs

3 tbsp whipping cream

Nutmeg

1 onion, sliced

2 tbsp olive oil

⅔ cup / 100 g frozen peas

1 tbsp chopped fresh basil

Salt and freshly ground pepper

Method

Cook and prep time: 40 min

1. Preheat the oven to 425° F (220°C / Gas Mark 7).

2. Boil the potatoes in salted water for about 20 minutes or until they can be easily pierced with a knife. Allow to cool. Peel and cut into bite-size pieces.

3. Rinse and coarsely chop the spinach.

4. Whisk the eggs with the cream. Season with salt, pepper and nutmeg.

5. Sauté the onion slices in hot oil. Add the potatoes and continue to sauté until golden brown, about 2–3 minutes.

6. Add the peas, spinach and basil. Pour in the eggs. Cook briefly, then place in the preheated oven for about 8 minutes until set.

Mushroom Flatbread

Ingredients

¾ oz / 20 g fresh yeast

1 pinch sugar

2½ cups / 250 g all-purpose (plain) flour

Salt

Butter, to grease the baking tray

For the topping:

5 oz / 150 g button mushrooms, sliced

2 shallots, sliced

Olive oil

Salt & freshly milled pepper

5 oz / 150 g goat cheese

½ bunch arugula (rocket) leaves

Method

Prep and cook time: 40 mins plus 45 mins rising time

1. For the dough, put the yeast into a large bowl with about ½ cup (125 ml) warm water and the sugar and mix smoothly. Then add the flour and salt and knead well until the dough is no longer sticky. Cover with a kitchen towel and put to rise in a warm place for 45 minutes, by which time it should have doubled in volume.

2. Preheat the oven to 425°F (220°C / Gas Mark 7). Knead the dough again (not too vigorously) on a floured work surface, then roll out thinly into 4 flatbreads and put on a greased cookie sheet.

3. Thinly slice the goat cheese and spread over the dough, then bake in the hot oven for about 15 minutes.

4. Heat 2 tablespoons olive oil and quickly sauté the mushrooms and shallots over a high heat. Season with salt and pepper, then remove from the heat.

5. Take the flatbread out of the oven, scatter evenly with the mushrooms, shallots and arugula (rocket) and served sprinkled with a little olive oil.

Pizza Margherita

Ingredients

For the base:

1½ tsp easy-bake yeast

¼ tsp sugar

1 lb / 450 g all-purpose (plain) flour

2 tbsp olive oil

1 tsp salt

For the topping:

4 tbsp olive oil, plus extra for drizzling

1 garlic clove, chopped

1 shallot, chopped

2 cups / 400 g canned tomatoes, chopped

2 tbsp tomato paste (purée)

1 tsp dried oregano

2 cups / 400 g mozzarella cheese

2 fresh tomatoes, sliced

Some black olives

Salt and freshly ground pepper

Method

Prep and cook time: 40 mins plus 1 hour rising time

1. Mix the yeast in a bowl with about 1/3 cup lukewarm water and the sugar.

2. Add the flour, olive oil and salt and knead to a pliable dough, adding a little water if the dough is too dry. Cover and put to rise in a warm place for about 1 hour.

3. Preheat the oven to 425°F (220°C / Gas Mark 7).

4. Heat some oil in a pan and sauté the garlic and shallot until translucent.

5. Add the canned tomatoes and tomato paste (purée) and stew gently for about 20 minutes. Season with oregano, salt and pepper.

6. Divide the dough into 4 and roll out on a lightly floured surface into circles of approximately 22 cm / 9 inch diameter, leaving the edges a little thicker.

7. Put the pizza bases on 2 greased cookie sheets and spread with the tomato sauce. Slice the mozzarella thinly and lay on the pizzas. Drizzle with a little olive oil.

8. Bake in the preheated oven for about 20 minutes. Take out and top with fresh tomato slices, oregano and olives. Serve immediately.

Omelette Wraps with Ham

Ingredients

4 tbsp butter

8 eggs, beaten

½ lb / 200 g thinly sliced ham

Lettuce leaves, thinly sliced

2 medium carrots, peeled and cut into thin strips

Salt and freshly ground pepper, to taste

Method

Prep and cook time: 25 min

1. Heat 1 tablespoon of the butter in an 8-inch (20-cm) nonstick skillet (frying pan) and pour in quarter of the egg mixture, swirling to coat the pan. When the eggs have set, transfer the omelet to a plate and repeat with the remaining butter and eggs to make four omelettes.

2. Arrange the ham, lettuce and carrot strips over the omelettes; season with salt and pepper and roll up to form a wrap. Slice in half along the diagonal and serve.

Bean and Cheese Quesadillas

Ingredients

1 tbsp vegetable oil

7 oz / 200 g bacon, diced

2 mild green chili peppers, sliced into rings

1 clove garlic, minced

1 tbsp tomato paste

1 (14 oz / 400 g) can red kidney beans, rinsed and drained

Salt, to taste

Cayenne pepper, to taste

4 flour tortillas

Scant 1 cup / 100 g shredded cheddar cheese

Method

Prep and cook time: 25 min

1. Preheat the oven to 400°F (200°C / Gas Mark 6). Line a baking sheet with foil or parchment.

2. Heat the oil in a skillet; add the bacon, chilies and garlic and fry until the bacon is cooked through. Stir in the tomato paste and 3–4 tablespoons water; add the beans and simmer, stirring, 2–3 minutes. Season with salt and cayenne pepper.

3. Spread the bean mixture onto the tortillas, top with cheese and fold in half. Place on a cookie sheet lined with parchment paper and bake until golden brown, about 10 minutes.

Egg and Tomato Wraps

Ingredients

1 large boiling (waxy) potato, cooked

4 eggs, hard boiled

¼ cup / 80 g salad cream or mayonnaise, more if required

1–2 tbsp mustard, medium strength

1–2 tbsp white wine vinegar

2–3 tbsp sour cream

2 tomatoes, cubed

1 red bell pepper, de-seeded and cubed

2 scallions (spring onions), trimmed and cut into rings

4–6 large wholewheat tortillas

Salt & freshly milled pepper

Method

Prep and cook time: 25 min

1. Dice the potato. Peel the eggs and cut into halves. Remove the egg yolks and mix to a smooth paste together with the salad cream (or mayonnaise), mustard, white wine vinegar and sour cream. Season to taste with salt and pepper. Cut the egg whites into small cubes.

2. Add the tomatoes, bell pepper, potatoes, egg whites and scallions to the egg and salad cream dressing and mix well. Spread the tomato and egg salad on top of the tortillas and roll up into a wrap. Cut in half, season with freshly milled pepper and serve in a bowl.

Chicken Salad Pitas

Ingredients

1 small grilled or roasted chicken

Scant 1 cup / 200 g mayonnaise

Scant ½ cup / 100 g sour cream

½ bunch parsley (about 1 oz / 25 g), chopped (reserve a few whole leaves for garnish)

1 red onion, coarsely chopped

1 tart green apple, cored, cut into eighths, and thinly sliced

1 clove garlic, minced

Salt and freshly ground pepper, to taste

4 pita breads, halved and split to make pockets

4–6 lettuce leaves

Method

Prep and cook time: 30 min

1. Skin the chicken, take the meat off the bone and shred or cut the meat into small pieces.

2. Combine in a bowl with the mayonnaise, sour cream, parsley, onion, apple and garlic; season with salt and pepper. Line the pita pockets with lettuce leaves, then stuff with the salad. Serve at once, garnished with parsley leaves.

Pancakes Stuffed with Smoked Salmon

Ingredients

For the pancakes:

Scant 2 cups / 200 g all-purpose (plain) flour

1⅔ cups / 400 ml milk

4 eggs

1 pinch salt

Butter, as needed for frying

For the filling:

About 1¼ cups / 300 g crème fraîche

1 tbsp lemon juice

Salt and freshly ground pepper, to taste

16 large slices smoked salmon

16 sage leaves (reserve additional leaves to garnish)

⅓ cup / 50 g toasted pine nuts

¾ cup / 100 g shredded Emmental cheese

Method

Prep and cook time: 45 min plus standing time: 30 min

1. Preheat the oven to 300°F (150° C / Gas Mark 2). Line a baking sheet with foil or parchment.

2. In a large bowl, whisk together the flour, milk, and salt; beat in the eggs one at a time. Let the batter stand for 30 minutes. Add a little more milk if the batter is too thick.

3. Heat a little butter in a skillet (frying pan) over medium heat; pour batter to make small pancakes. Cook, turning once, until lightly browned on both sides; transfer to a plate and continue with the remaining batter to make about 16 pancakes.

4. In a small bowl, blend the crème fraîche and lemon juice until smooth and season with salt and pepper.

5. Spread each pancake with a dollop of crème fraîche mixture; top with a slice of salmon, a sage leaf, and a sprinkle of pine nuts; roll up. Sprinkle with the cheese and place on the baking sheet; bake until the cheese melts. Slice in half at an angle and serve on plates, garnished with sage leaves.

Potato Pancakes
with Smoked Salmon and Soured Cream

Ingredients

For the potato pancake batter:

¼ lb / 100 g potatoes, cubed

2 eggs

7 tbsp milk

1 cup / 100 g all-purpose (plain) flour

2 tbsp butter

Salt and freshly ground pepper

To serve:

8 slices smoked salmon

Generous ½ cup / 150 g soured cream

Method

Prep and cook time: 25 min

1. Put the potatoes into a pan of salted water and bring to a boil. Cover and simmer for 15 minutes until the potatoes are tender. Drain, return to the pan and mash until really smooth. Cool for a few minutes.

2. Beat the eggs together with the milk in a jug. Gradually pour the egg mixture into the potatoes to make a smooth batter.

3. Mix in the flour and season with salt and ground pepper.

4. Melt a knob of butter in a pan and drop in a couple of ladlefuls of batter, well spaced apart – the pancake should be quite thick.

5. Cook the pancakes for a couple of minutes each side until golden.

6. Remove from the pan and keep warm while you cook the rest of the mixture.

7. Serve the pancakes with smoked salmon and soured cream, seasoned with a pinch of sea salt and ground pepper.

Whitebait with Caper Dip

Ingredients

For the whitebait:

Vegetable oil, for deep frying

2 lbs / 900 g whitebait

4 tbsp all-purpose (plain) flour

¼ tsp cayenne pepper

Salt & black pepper

For the lemon caper mayo:

²/₃ cup / 150 ml   mayonnaise

1 lemon, finely grated zest and juice

¹/₃ cup / 50 g capers, drained

¹/₃ cup / 50 g baby gherkins, chopped

1 lemon, cut into 6 wedges, to garnish

Method

Prep and cook time: 30 min

1. Half fill a deep fat fryer or large heavy-based saucepan with oil and heat to 170°C /325°F.

2. Mix together the mayonnaise, lemon zest, juice of ½ the lemon, capers and gherkins. Add more lemon juice to taste.

3. Wash the whitebait and pat dry with paper towels.

4. Put the flour into a large zip bag with plenty of salt, ground black pepper and the cayenne.

5. Add the whitebait, seal the bag and toss together so that the fish becomes coated in the flour.

6. Deep fry a couple of handfuls of the whitebait for 2–3 minutes, until crisp. Drain on paper towels and repeat with the rest of the fish.

7. Season with salt and serve with the lemon and caper mayo and garnished with lemon wedges.

MAIN COURSES

Braised Beef Pot Roast
with Vegetables

Ingredients

2¼ lb / 1 kg beef

2 fennel bulbs

2 celery sticks

2 onions

2 carrots

2 parsnips

Salt & freshly milled pepper

4 tbsp oil

2 oz / 50 g bacon, diced

2 cups / 500 ml beef broth (stock)

3–4 allspice berries, crushed

10 peppercorns, crushed

2 bay leaves

Method
Prep and cook time: 3 hours

1. Wash the fennel bulbs, remove any tough outer layers and the core and slice thinly.

2. Wash and clean the celery and cut diagonally into pieces.

3. Wash and peel the onions, the carrots and the parsnips and chop.

4. Wash the beef, pat dry and season all over with salt and pepper.

5. Fry the beef in hot oil on all sides in a flameproof casserole, then remove and set aside.

6. Fry the bacon in the remaining oil, add the onion and the vegetables and sauté until browned.

7. Add the crushed allspice berries and the peppercorns as well as the bay leaves and pour in some of the beef broth (stock). Put the beef on top of the vegetables, cover and braise for about 2–2½ hours over a low heat until tender.

8. Keep adding some of the beef broth and turning the beef every so often.

9. Season to taste with salt and pepper and serve.

Beef Goulash

Ingredients

2 lb / about 1 kg beef chuck, cubed

3 tbsp oil

4 onions

2 cloves garlic

1 tbsp paprika, sweet

½ tsp caraway seeds, ground

2 cups / 500 ml beef broth (stock)

Salt & freshly milled pepper

1 bay leaf

1 tsp paprika, hot

1 tbsp marjoram leaves, fresh

Method
Prep and cook time: 1 hour 45 min

1. Fry the beef on all sides in hot oil, a few pieces at a time, until browned.

2. Peel the onion and the garlic. Cut the onions in half, then into slices. Chop the garlic.

3. Reduce the heat and sauté the onions together with the meat.

4. Add the sweet paprika and the ground caraway, then pour in the beef broth (stock). Now add the bay leaf, the garlic and the hot paprika.

5. Simmer over a low heat for about 1–1½ hours, stirring occasionally. Add a little water if necessary.

6. When cooked, season to taste with salt and pepper and sprinkle a few marjoram leaves over the top. Serve with bread or boiled potatoes.

Beef Ragout
with Chanterelle Mushrooms

Ingredients

2¼ lbs / 1 kg beef chuck, chopped

3 onions

2 garlic cloves

2 tbsp flour

2–4 tbsp sunflower oil

Good ½ cup / 150 ml port wine

1 cup / 250 ml beef broth (stock)

Salt & freshly milled pepper

1 bay leaf

14 oz / 400 g chanterelle mushrooms

1 tbsp / 25 g butter

2 tbsp chopped parsley

Method
Prep and cook time: 2 h

1. Peel and finely chop the onions and garlic.

2. Coat the meat with flour and fry in hot oil, a few pieces at a time. Remove from the pan and fry the onions and the garlic until browned.

3. Add the meat again and pour in the port wine. Pour in some of the beef broth (stock) and season with salt, pepper and the bay leaf.

4. Cover with a lid and cook on a low heat for about 1½ hours, stirring occasionally. Add a little broth if needed.

5. In the meantime clean the chanterelle mushrooms and fry in hot butter. Season with salt and pepper.

6. When the ragout is cooked, add the chanterelle mushrooms and stir. Sprinkle the chopped parsley over the top and serve.

Chili Beef
with Winter Vegetables

Ingredients

1lb 6 oz / 600 g beef, for stewing (such as from the leg)

1lb 6 oz / 600 g baking potatoes

1⅓ cups / 200 g chickpeas (garbanzo beans), canned, drained

2 onions

2 cloves garlic

5 tomatoes

3–4 tbsp sunflower oil

A pinch of curry powder

¼ tsp cayenne pepper

½ tsp ground cumin

1¾ cups / 400 ml meat broth (stock)

1¾ cups / 200 g frozen peas

Salt

2 tbsp pumpkin seeds

Method
Prep and cook time: 1 hour 30 min

1. Wash and dry the beef and cut into cubes. Peel and roughly dice the potatoes. Rinse the chickpeas (garbanzo beans).

2. Peel and chop the onions and garlic. Drop the tomatoes into boiling water for a few seconds, refresh in cold water, then skin, quarter, de-seed and dice.

3. Heat the oil and brown the meat on all sides. Add the onions and garlic and fry briefly, then add the curry powder, cayenne pepper and cumin. Add the broth (stock), cover and stew for about 30 minutes.

4. Add the potatoes, tomatoes, chickpeas and peas and simmer gently for a further 40–50 minutes. Stir occasionally and add more broth if necessary. Season to taste.

5. Toast the pumpkin seeds in a dry skillet. Serve scattered with pumpkin seeds.

Beef and Vegetable Stew

Ingredients

1¼ lb / 500 g beef, for braising
(such as chuck)

2 chicory heads (endives)

2 carrots

1 zucchini (courgette)

8 oz / 250 g celery root (celeriac)

2 onions

2 cloves garlic

3 tbsp sunflower oil

1¾ cups / 400 ml beef broth (stock)

7 oz / 200 g broccoli florets

Salt & freshly milled pepper

1 tbsp chopped parsley

Fresh sage leaves, to garnish

Method

Prep and cook time: 1 hour 20 min

1. Wash the beef, pat dry with paper towel and cut into cubes.

2. Wash and trim the chicory (endives), then cut into wedges. Peel the carrots and cut into short lengths. Wash, trim and chop the zucchini (courgette).

3. Peel the celery root (celeriac) and roughly chop. Peel the onions and the garlic and finely chop.

4. Fry the meat in hot oil until browned on all sides. Add the onions and the garlic and fry until lightly browned.

5. Now add the carrots, endives, celery root and sauté the vegetables.

6. Pour in the broth (stock), bring to a boil, cover and simmer for about 30 minutes. Now add the broccoli florets and the zucchini and simmer for a further 30 minutes until cooked.

7. Season to taste with salt and pepper, sprinkle chopped parsley over the top, garnish with sage leaves and serve.

Greek Stifado

Ingredients

2¼ lbs / 1 kg beef, from the leg, without bones

6 tbsp olive oil

Salt & freshly milled pepper

2 cloves garlic

3 bay leaves

1 cinnamon stick

½ tsp nutmeg, grated

½ tsp cinnamon, ground

½ tsp cumin, ground

2 tbsp tomato concentrate or passata

3 tbsp red wine vinegar

1½ cups / 250 g tomato paste (purée)

2 cups / 500 ml water

Scant ½ cup / 100 ml red wine

about 2 lb / 1 kg small onions

14 oz / 400 g small tomatoes

2 tbsp chopped parsley

Method

Prep and cook time: 2 hours 20 min

1. Wash the beef, pat dry with paper towel and cut into about 1 inch (2 cm) cubes.

2. Heat the oil in a flameproof casserole and fry the meat until browned on all sides, a few pieces at a time. Season with salt and pepper then take out of the casserole.

3. Peel and finely chop the garlic. Add the garlic, bay leaves, cinnamon stick, nutmeg, cinnamon, cumin and tomato concentrate or passata and sauté, stirring continually.

4. Put the meat back in the casserole and stir. Pour in the red wine vinegar and simmer for 2–3 minutes.

5. Now add the tomato paste (purée) and the water (the meat should be just about covered). Pour in the wine, cover with a lid and simmer for 1 hour.

6. Put the small onions in boiling water and leave for about 1 minute. Drain, put under cold water and peel. Put the onions in the casserole and simmer for another 1 hour.

7. Put the tomatoes in hot water for a few seconds, then immediately into cold water and peel.

8. Put the tomatoes in the casserole about 5 minutes before the end of cooking time. Season to taste and stir in the chopped parsley.

Lancashire Hotpot

Ingredients

1¼ lb / 500 g beef

1 onion

2 carrots

1 stick of celery

1 lb 6 oz / 600 g potatoes

1 tbsp / 20 g butter

Marjoram

Salt & freshly milled pepper

3 cups / 750 ml broth (stock)

Method

Prep and cook time: 1 hour 45 min

1. Preheat the oven to 200°C (400°F / Gas Mark 6). Wash the meat, pat dry with paper towel and cut into smallish cubes.

2. Wash, trim, peel and finely dice the vegetables (apart from the potatoes).

3. Peel the potatoes and slice thinly, using a mandolin vegetable slicer, if available.

4. Butter a casserole dish and put all the ingredients into it in layers, beginning with a layer of potatoes, then marjoram and seasoning, vegetables and meat. Finish with a neat layer of potatoes and season again.

5. Pour the broth (stock) over, cover and cook in the oven for about 90 minutes. Shortly before the end of cooking time remove the lid to brown the potatoes.

Cottage Pie

Ingredients

1 tbsp olive oil

2 onions, chopped

1 lb / 450 g ground beef

2 cups / 450 ml beef broth (stock)

1 tbsp all-purpose (plain) flour

1 tbsp Worcestershire sauce

1 tbsp tomato purée

Salt and freshly ground pepper, to taste

2 lb / 900 g potatoes, peeled and cut into chunks

1 tbsp / 25 g butter

4 tbsp milk

Method

Prep and cook time: 1 hour 10 min

1. Heat the oven to 170°C (325°F / Gas Mark 3).

2. Heat the oil in a large flameproof casserole and fry the onions for 5 minutes until softened.

3. Add the beef and cook, stirring, until well browned. Stir in the broth (stock), flour, Worcestershire sauce, and tomato purée. Bring to a boil and season with salt and pepper. Cover and carefully transfer to the oven. Bake for about 20 minutes, until tender.

4. Meanwhile, put the potatoes into a saucepan with enough salted water to cover. Bring to a boil, reduce heat and simmer for 20–25 minutes until very tender.

5. Drain the potatoes, return to the pan, and mash until very smooth. Beat in the butter and milk.

6. Increase the oven temperature to 220°C (400°F / Gas Mark 6.)

7. Spoon the beef into a 1½-quart (1.7 liter) baking dish. Spread the potato mixture on top, to completely cover the meat. Place on a baking sheet and bake for 25 minutes until the top is starting to brown.

Meatloaf

Ingredients

1 tbsp oil

1 lb / 450 g lean ground (minced) beef

1 onion, finely chopped

1 garlic clove, finely chopped

1 tbsp red wine vinegar

1 tbsp tomato paste (purée)

1 cup / 50 g fresh white breadcrumbs

Salt, to taste

Method

Prep and cook time: 1 hour 15 min

1. Preheat the oven to 350°F (180°C / Gas Mark 4).

2. Mix all the ingredients together until well combined.

3. Pack firmly into a greased loaf tin and cover with foil.

4. Bake for about 1 hour, until completely cooked through. Serve warm or cold.

Meat Patties
with Onions and Tomatoes

Ingredients

3 oz / 80 g white bread, crusts removed

1/3 cup / 80 ml milk

1 onion, finely chopped

1 tbsp butter

1¾ cups / 400 g mixed ground meat

2 eggs

1 tbsp hot mustard

1 chili, chopped

1 tsp dried marjoram

2 tbsp chopped fresh parsley

Breadcrumbs

Salt & freshly milled pepper

Oil, for brushing

4 tomatoes, quartered

2 red onions, cut into thick rings

Herbs, to garnish

Method

Prep and cook time: 30 min

1. For the meat patties, soak the bread in the milk. Heat the butter in a skillet and sauté the onion over a low heat until translucent.

2. Mix the ground meat with the soaked bread, eggs, mustard, chili, and onion. Add the marjoram and parsley and as many breadcrumbs as necessary to produce a shapeable mixture. Season with salt and pepper.

3. Shape into patties, brush with oil, and grill for 2–3 minutes each side. Sprinkle the red onions and tomatoes with a little oil and put on the grill with the patties.

4. Put the meat patties on plates with the tomatoes and onions. Garnish with herbs and serve with boiled new potatoes.

Lasagne

Ingredients

7 oz / 200 g lasagne sheets (no pre-cook type)

For the Bolognese sauce:

1 onion

2 cloves garlic

1 carrot

3 stalks celery

5oz / 150 g mozzarella

3 tbsp olive oil

8 oz / 250 g mixed pork and beef ground meat

2 tbsp tomato paste (purée)

¼ cup / 50 ml red wine

14 oz / 400 g can chopped tomatoes

Salt & freshly milled pepper

²/₃ cup / 80g Parmesan cheese, freshly grated

For the béchamel sauce:

4 tbsp / 60 g butter

3–4 tbps / 50 g all-purpose (plain) flour

2 cups / 500 ml milk

Method

Prep and cook time: 1 h 30 min

1. Peel the onion and the garlic and finely chop. Peel and trim the carrot and the celery and finely chop. Cut the mozzarella into thin slices.

2. Heat the olive oil in a skillet and fry the onions, garlic and ground meat. Add the carrots and the celery and sauté. Stir in the tomato paste (purée) and pour in the red wine and chopped tomatoes. Season with salt and pepper, and then simmer for about 20 minutes.

3. For the béchamel sauce, melt 3½ tbsp (50 g) of the butter in a pan. Stir in the flour and cook over a low heat. Gradually add the milk, stirring continually, and then season to taste with salt and pepper. Simmer gently for 5 minutes, stirring continually.

4. Preheat the oven to 400°F (200°C / Gas Mark 6).

5. Spoon 2–3 tablespoons of béchamel sauce into a baking dish. Place a layer of lasagne sheets on top, followed by a layer of the Bolognese sauce. Repeat the process, and then finish with a layer of lasagne sheets and top with the remaining béchamel sauce. Cover the top with a layer of mozzarella slices and grated Parmesan cheese. Put a few knobs of butter on the top and then bake in the oven for about 40 minutes until cooked.

Steak
with Mozzarella and Grapefruit

Ingredients

1 grapefruit

2 avocados

4 (5-6 oz / about 160 g) steaks, (e. g. rib eye or sirloin)

4 tbsp olive oil, divided

1 lb / 400 g cherry tomatoes

8 mild red chili peppers

1 clove garlic, minced

About 1 lb / 400 g mini mozzarella balls, drained

Salt and freshly ground black pepper, to taste

Method
Prep and cook time: 40 min

1. Turn the broiler (grill) to high.

2. Peel the grapefruit and remove the segments, avoiding the pith and membrane, reserving the juice. Peel and halve the avocados, remove the pits and roughly dice the flesh. Sprinkle with half of the grapefruit juice.

3. Pat dry the steaks, rub them with a little of the oil and place under the broiler (grill). Cook for 3–5 minutes on each side depending on preference and the thickness of the meat. Wrap the meat in foil and set aside.

4. Return the skillet to the heat and sauté the tomatoes, chilies and garlic until softened. Add the remaining grapefruit juice, remove from the heat and add the avocado, mozzarella and grapefruit segments. Toss to combine and season to taste with salt and pepper.

5. Season the meat with salt and pepper. Cut each piece in halves or thirds and put on warmed plates. Add the vegetables and mozzarella and serve.

Spaghetti
with Meatballs and Tomato Sauce

Ingredients

12 oz / 350 g spaghetti

For the meatballs:

1 slice stale white bread

3 tbsp cream

14 oz / 400 g ground beef

1 egg

2 tbsp chopped fresh parsley

Lemon zest

Salt & freshly milled pepper

Butter

For the tomato sauce:

1 clove garlic

2 shallots

4 tbsp olive oil

1 tsp tomato paste (purée)

14 oz / 400 g can chopped tomatoes

Salt & freshly milled pepper

½ tsp sugar

Fresh parsley, to garnish

Method

Prep and cook time: 40 min

1. For the meatballs, roughly chop the bread and soak it in cream until soft. Squeeze the bread to remove excess cream, and then mix together with the ground beef, egg, chopped parsley and lemon zest. Season with salt and pepper and mix well. Form small balls from the mix.

2. For the tomato sauce, peel and finely chop the garlic and the shallots. Fry in hot olive oil in a saucepan until soft. Stir in the tomato paste (purée), followed by the chopped tomatoes. Simmer gently for about 20 minutes. Season with salt, pepper and sugar.

3. Cook the spaghetti in boiling, salted water according to instructions on the packet.

4. Fry the meatballs in butter for 6–8 minutes on all sides. Drain the spaghetti and divide onto plates, arrange the meatballs on the top and spoon some of the tomato sauce over everything. Garnish with parsley and serve.

Spaghetti Bolognese

Ingredients

10 oz / 300 g lean ground beef

1 tbsp olive oil

1 onion, chopped

1 carrot, chopped

2 roasted red bell peppers, drained

14 oz / 400 g can plum tomatoes

2 dashes Worcestershire sauce

12 oz / 350 g spaghetti

Basil leaves, to garnish

Method

Prep and cook time: 40 min

1. Fry the beef in a large nonstick skillet for 15 minutes, until browned.

2. Heat the oil in a large skillet, add the onion and fry gently for 5 minutes, to soften. Add the carrot; cook for 5 minutes to soften.

3. Chop the peppers and add it to the carrot and onion. Stir in the tomatoes and their juice, and cook for 5 minutes more.

4. Add the tomato sauce and Worcestershire sauce to the beef. Add ½ cup / 100 ml water, stir, cover and simmer for 10 minutes.

5. Meanwhile, bring a large pot of salted water to a boil, add the spaghetti and cook according to package instructions, for about 10 minutes, until al dente.

6. Drain the pasta and divide between 4 plates. Top with the beef mixture and garnish with basil leaves.

Pad Thai

Ingredients

8 oz / 250 g dried rice noodles

2 tbsp oil

3 cloves garlic, chopped

2 tsp red chilies, chopped

14 oz / 400 g beef, for pan-frying, cut into thin strips

2 tbsp fish sauce

2 tbsp lime juice

2 tsp brown sugar

¼ cup / 40 g soybean sprouts

¼ cup / 40 g frozen peas

¼ cup / 40 g soybeans, canned

Green scallion (spring onion) stalks, to garnish

Method

Prep and cook time: 20 min plus 10 min soaking time

1. Soak the noodles in warm water for 10 minutes, then drain and set aside.

2. Heat the oil in a wok or a large skillet. Add the garlic, chilies and beef and stir-fry for about 4 minutes. Add the drained noodles, cover and fry for a further minute.

3. Add the fish sauce, lime juice and sugar and stir well until everything is heated evenly. Add the soybean sprouts, peas and soybeans and cook until done.

4. Check the seasoning and serve garnished with the green stalks of the scallion (spring onion) cut into rings.

Beef with Black Beans

Ingredients

3 tbsp toasted sesame oil, divided

8 shallots, quartered

2 inch / 5 cm piece fresh ginger root, peeled and thinly sliced

2 cloves garlic, thinly sliced

1 head broccoli, stems peeled and cut into small florets

2 heads bok choy, quartered lengthwise

12 oz / 300 g rump steak, thinly sliced

1/3 cup / 150 g black bean stir-fry sauce

Method

Prep and cook time: 20 min

1. Heat 2 tablespoons of the oil in a large skillet (frying pan) over medium heat. Add the shallots, ginger and garlic and stir-fry for 2 minutes or until just beginning to color.

2. Add the broccoli and bok choy and stir-fry for 2–3 minutes until wilted, but still crisp. Divide between four plates or bowls and keep warm.

3. Heat the remaining tablespoon of oil in the skillet over high heat. Add the steak and cook, turning occasionally, for 2 minutes or until well browned and cooked to your liking. Reduce the heat.

4. Pour the black bean sauce over the top and add 5 tablespoons of cold water. Cook, stirring gently for 1 minute until the beef is well coated and the sauce is hot. Spoon over the vegetables and serve immediately.

Beef with Mushrooms and Cabbage

Ingredients

2 tbsp vegetable oil

12 oz / 300 g lean beef steak, sliced

½ Chinese cabbage (leaves), sliced

1 red bell pepper, sliced into strips

12 oz / 300 g Asian mushrooms (try straw, oyster, shiitake or enoki), sliced if large

2 tsp cornstarch (cornflour)

2 tsp dry sherry

2 tsp dark soy sauce

½ cup / 100 ml beef broth (stock)

Method

Prep and cook time: 20 min

1. Heat the oil in a large wok or skillet, add the beef and stir-fry just until browned, 3 minutes. Add the cabbage and bell pepper and stir-fry 1 minute. Add the mushrooms and cook for 2 minutes more; set aside and keep warm.

2. In a small bowl, mix the cornstarch with the sherry to a smooth paste.

3. In a medium saucepan, combine the broth (stock) and soy sauce; stir in the cornstarch mixture. Bring to a boil and cook, stirring, until the sauce is thickened.

4. Add the sauce to the beef and vegetables; heat through and serve at once.

Lamb Stew
with Dumplings

Ingredients

1 lb 6 oz / 600 g lamb, for braising

2 onions

2 cloves garlic

2 stalks celery

7 oz / 200 g potatoes

7 oz / 200 g sweet potatoes

2 carrots

2 tbsp sunflower oil

2¼ cups / 600 ml beef broth (stock)

Salt & freshly milled pepper

2 bay leaves

For the dumplings:

2 cups / 200 g all-purpose (plain) flour

1 egg

1 tbsp thyme leaves, dried

Scant ½ cup / 100 ml milk

Grated nutmeg

Method
Prep and cook time: 1 hour 20 min

1. Wash the lamb, pat dry with paper towel then cut into cubes.

2. Peel the onions and the garlic and chop. Wash and trim the celery, then chop.

3. Peel the potatoes and sweet potatoes, then cut into cubes. Peel the carrots, cut in half lengthways, then chop.

4. Fry the meat in hot oil until browned on all sides. Add the onions and the garlic and pour in the broth (stock). Season and bring to a boil then simmer for about 30 minutes.

5. Add all the vegetables and bay leaves and simmer for a further 45 minutes.

6. In the meantime make the dumplings. Mix the flour, egg and thyme and add enough milk to form a dough.

7. Season with salt and freshly grated nutmeg. Use a teaspoon to form tiny balls, then place in boiling, salted water and simmer for about 10 minutes.

8. Season the stew with salt and pepper and serve with a few dumplings.

Irish Stew with Savoy Cabbage

Ingredients

1 lb 12 oz / 800 g lamb, from the leg

1 small savoy cabbage

14 oz / 400 g potatoes

1 leek

2 carrots

2 onions

Salt & freshly milled pepper

1 pinch caraway seeds, ground (optional)

1 bunch flat-leaf parsley

1 bay leaf

3½ cups / 900 ml beef broth (stock)

½ lemon, grated zest

Method

Prep and cook time: 2 hours 30 min

1. Pre-heat the oven to 325°F (170°C / Gas Mark 3).

2. Cut the fat off the meat and cut into about 1 inch / 3 cm cubes. Clean the savoy cabbage, quarter, remove the core and roughly shred. Wash and scrub the potatoes and cut into dice.

3. Wash and clean the leek and cut diagonally into slices. Peel the carrots and cut into slices. Peel and finely chop the onions.

4. Put a layer of savoy cabbage on the bottom of a casserole, followed by some lamb and onions. Season with salt, pepper and ground caraway.

5. Add a layer of potatoes, leek and carrots and season again. Carry on layering the casserole until all ingredients have been used up. Finish with a layer of vegetables.

6. Put half the parsley and the bay leaf on the top. Pour in the broth (stock), cover and put on the lower shelf of the oven

7. Cook for about 1½ hours, then open the lid and remove the bay leaf and the parsley. Cook for a further 30 minutes without the lid.

8. Adjust the seasoning, sprinkle the remaining chopped parsley and lemon zest over the top and serve.

Lamb Stew
with Peas and Potatoes

Ingredients

1 lb 2 oz / 500 g lamb pieces

2 tbsp olive oil

2 tbsp tomato paste (purée)

4 cups / 1 liter vegetable broth (stock)

1 pack of soup vegetables (including, for example, carrot, leek, celery, parsnip, turnip) – about 1lb / 450 g

8–10 shallots

1 bay leaf

Salt & freshly milled pepper

1 lb / 450 g potatoes

3 carrots

A few sprigs of marjoram

1 tsp dried savory

2½ cups / 300 g frozen peas

1 tbsp flour

1 tbsp / 20 g butter

Method

Prep and cook time: 1 hour

1. Heat the oil in a large pan and brown the meat on all sides. Add the tomato paste (purée) and vegetable broth (stock) and bring to a boil.

2. Meanwhile prepare the soup vegetables and chop very finely. Peel the shallots and cut off the roots.

3. Skim off any scum from the meat broth with a skimmer and add the soup vegetables, shallots, bay leaf and seasoning to the meat. Cover and simmer for about 40 minutes.

4. Meanwhile peel the potatoes and carrots. Halve or quarter the potatoes and cut the carrots into ¾ inch (2 cm) lengths. Add to the meat after 10 minutes cooking time and simmer until the meat is tender.

5. Finely chop the marjoram. About 10 minutes before the end of cooking time add the marjoram, savory and frozen peas to the stew.

6. Blend the flour and butter into a paste, stir into the stew and bring to a boil. Allow to thicken slightly, then check the seasoning, remove the bay leaf and serve.

Lamb Rogan Josh

Ingredients

6 cloves garlic

1 tsp freshly grated ginger

6 tbsp oil

8 cardamom seeds

1 inch / 2.5 cm cinnamon stick

2 bay leaves

1 lb 12 oz /800 g lamb, from the leg, cut into bite-size pieces

2 onions, chopped

1–2 tsp cumin

1–2 tsp ground coriander

½ tsp cayenne pepper, according to taste

1 tbsp sweet paprika

1–2 tbsp tomato paste (purée)

Salt

Method

Prep and cook time: 1 hour 20 min

1. Peel the garlic and crush in a garlic press. Mix the garlic with the freshly grated ginger.

2. Heat the oil in a large skillet (frying pan). Fry the cardamom, cinnamon and bay leaves in the oil, then add the meat and fry until browned on all sides.

3. Take the meat out of the skillet and fry the onions, then add the garlic–ginger mixture. Now add the cumin, coriander, cayenne pepper, paprika and tomato paste (purée) and stir. Add the meat, season to taste with salt and pour in 1¼ cups / 300 ml water.

4. Bring to a boil and simmer gently for about 1 hour. Serve with rice.

Jalfrezi
(Anglo-Indian Curry)

Ingredients

About 1 lb / 500 g roasted meat, lamb or beef (leftover meat is ideal)

3 onions

3 tomatoes

3 green chilies

3 tbsp sunflower oil

¼ tsp mustard seeds

¼ tsp cumin seeds

¼ tsp coriander, ground

¼ tsp curcuma (turmeric), ground

1 tbsp Worcestershire sauce

Salt & freshly milled pepper

Parsley, to garnish

Method

Prep and cook time: 30 min

1. Cut the meat into thin strips. Peel the onions, cut in half, then into thin slices.

2. Put the tomatoes in boiling water for a few seconds, then immediately into cold water. Skin, quarter, de-seed the tomatoes and finely chop.

3. Wash the chilies, cut in half lengthways, de-seed and finely chop.

4. Heat the oil in a skillet (frying pan) and toast the mustard and cumin seeds for about 30 seconds, stirring continually.

5. Add the onions and the chilies and fry until slightly browned, stirring continually.

6. Add the meat, the ground spices, the Worcestershire sauce and the tomatoes. Season with salt and pepper and cook on a medium heat for about 3–5 minutes, stirring continuously.

7. Garnish with parsley and serve with rice.

Lamb Korma

Ingredients

1 cup / 250 ml full-fat yogurt

1 tsp salt

2 tsp ground cumin

1 tsp ground coriander

A pinch of cayenne pepper

4 tbsp freshly chopped cilantro (coriander)

5 tbsp olive oil

1 bay leaf

6 cardamom pods

Cinnamon stick (2 inches / 5 cm)

2 lb / 900 g lamb, from the shoulder, without bones, cut into bite-size cubes

1 onion, chopped

4 tbsp golden raisins

2 tbsp sour cream

A pinch of ground cardamom

Freshly milled pepper

Method

Prep and cook time: 1 hour 20 min

1. Mix the yogurt with the salt, cumin, ground coriander, cayenne pepper, black pepper and fresh cilantro (coriander) leaves and set aside.

2. Heat the oil in a large skillet. When the oil is hot add the bay leaf, cardamom pods, cinnamon and diced meat. Brown the meat on all sides over a medium heat. If the skillet is not big enough to take all the meat at once, it is better to fry the meat a few pieces at a time so that it has plenty of room in the skillet.

3. Take the meat out of the skillet and keep warm. Sauté the onion until translucent in the oil left in the skillet.

4. Return the meat to the skillet with the spices, add the yogurt mixture and golden raisins and bring to a boil. Cover and cook over a low heat for 60–70 minutes, until the meat is very tender. Then remove the lid and cook over a high heat until the sauce is reduced to the desired consistency.

5. Stir in the sour cream, season with the ground cardamom and serve at once.

Lamb and Spinach Curry

Ingredients

2¼ lb / 1 kg lamb, shoulder or leg

3 onions

2 cloves garlic

1 piece fresh ginger, 1 inch / about 2.5 cm

2 red chilies, finely chopped

½ tsp paprika, noble sweet

A pinch of ground cloves

1 tsp curcuma (turmeric)

1 tsp ground coriander

Salt

¼ cup / 50 g yogurt

Scant 1 cup / about 200 ml lamb broth (stock)

7 oz / 200 g spinach

3 tbsp oil

2 tbsp chopped cilantro (coriander) leaves

Method

Prep and cook time: 1 hour 45 min plus 1 hour to marinate

1. Cut the meat into 1½-inch (4-cm) cubes. Peel the onions, halve lengthways and slice thinly. Peel the garlic and finely dice 1 clove.

2. Peel and grate the ginger. Press the remaining garlic clove into the ginger. Mix the ginger and garlic with the rest of the spices and ½ teaspoon salt, then add to the yogurt and mix well. Mix the meat with the yogurt marinade, cover and marinate in the refrigerator for about 1 hour.

3. Heat the oil in a skillet (frying pan). Gently sweat the onion slices for about 3 minutes before adding the diced garlic and sautéing for a further minute. Add the meat with the marinade. Cover and simmer over a low heat for about 1¼ hours, gradually adding the lamb stock and stirring frequently.

4. Wash and roughly chop the spinach and add to the lamb during the last 15 minutes of cooking time.

5. Check the seasoning and serve with rice.

Grilled Lamb Cutlets
with Tomatoes and Herb Butter

Ingredients

2 tomatoes, chopped

2 cloves garlic

8 tbsp olive oil

1 tsp freshly chopped thyme

1 tsp freshly chopped rosemary

Salt & freshly milled pepper

12 lamb cutlets, French trimmed, each weighing about 3 oz / 80 g

Tomato wedges, to garnish

Rosemary, to garnish

For the herb butter:

2½ oz / 5 tbsp / 75 g soft butter

Salt & freshly milled pepper

1–2 tbsp finely chopped herbs: parsley, chervil, tarragon

1 tsp lemon juice

1 clove garlic, finely chopped

Method

Prep and cook time: 20 min plus 12 hours marinating time

1. Mix the oil with the herbs, garlic, and chopped tomatoes and season with salt and pepper.

2. Wash and dry the lamb cutlets, put into the tomato and garlic marinade, cover and marinate overnight, turning once.

3. Cream the butter with the salt and pepper and mix with the herbs and lemon juice. Peel the garlic, press into the butter and stir in.

4. Shape the butter into a roll, wrap in aluminum foil and chill.

5. Heat the broiler (grill). Drain the lamb cutlets and cook on the hot grill for 2–3 minutes each side.

6. Sprinkle with marinade, arrange on plates and garnish with tomato wedges and rosemary. Add a few slices of the herb butter and serve.

Lamb Chops with Pesto

Ingredients

2 cups / 40 g basil leaves

2 garlic cloves

1 tbsp pine nuts

Olive oil

2 handfuls arugula (rocket)

8 lamb chops

Salt and freshly ground pepper

Method

Prep and cook time: 30 min

1. For the pesto, pick off the basil leaves and purée with the peeled garlic, pine nuts and sufficient oil to produce a creamy mixture, adding the oil in a steady stream. Season to taste with salt and pepper.

2. Wash and sort the arugula (rocket) and arrange on plates.

3. Wash and dry the chops and season with salt and pepper.

4. Heat a little oil and fry the chops for 2–3 minutes each side, or until golden brown.

5. Place two lamb chops on each plate and serve drizzled with pesto.

Lamb and Potato Salad

Ingredients

2 red bell peppers, cored and quartered lengthwise

1¼ lb / 600 g potatoes, peeled and quartered

Salt and freshly ground pepper, to taste

6–7 tbsp olive oil

1 tsp curry powder

1 lb / 500 g loin of lamb, trimmed of fat

2 tbsp lemon juice

2 tbsp wine vinegar

4 cups / 175 g baby salad greens or spring mix

8 oz / 200 g mini mozzarella balls

Method

Prep and cook time: 45 min

1. Season the potatoes with salt and pepper, scatter them in an oven dish and drizzle with a little olive oil.

2. Preheat the broiler (grill). Line a broiler pan with foil. Place the bell pepper pieces skin-side-up on the pan and broil (grill) until the skin blisters and blackens. Take out, cover with a damp cloth and let cool. Then skin and cut into strips.

3. Season the lamb with salt and pepper and rub with a little of the oil. Put under the hot grill for 3–5 minutes each side, depending on preference and the thickness of the meat. Wrap in foil and set aside.

4. Reduce the temperature to 350°F (180°C / Gas Mark 4) and bake the potatoes for 20–25 minutes, turning occasionally.

5. Mix the curry powder with 3 tablespoons of the oil in a small bowl and brush the mixture onto the potatoes. Continue baking for a further 10 minutes, or until tender.

6. In a large bowl, whisk the remaining 4 tablespoons oil, the lemon juice and vinegar to make a vinaigrette. Add the salad greens and gently toss to coat; season with salt and pepper. Divide between 4 bowls and add the mozzarella. Thinly slice the meat and put on top of the salad with the potatoes. Scatter with the pepper strips and serve at once.

Moroccan Lamb Kebabs with Yogurt Sauce

Ingredients

1lb 12 oz / 800 g lamb, from the leg

3 oz / 80 g mixed salad leaves

4 pita breads

1 lemon

8 wooden skewers

For the marinade:

Juice of 1 lemon

3–4 tbsp olive oil

2 sprigs rosemary, roughly chopped

½ inch / 1 cm fresh ginger, freshly grated

1 pinch cumin

1 chili pepper, finely chopped

For the yogurt sauce:

1 clove garlic

1 bunch parsley, roughly chopped

14 oz / 400 g natural yogurt

1 tsp lemon zest

Salt & white pepper

Method

Prep and cook time: 15 min plus 2 hours marinating time

1. Mix all the marinade ingredients and put into a freezer bag.

2. Cut the meat into ¾-inch (2-cm) cubes and put into the freezer bag with the marinade. Seal and knead to make sure the meat is coated in the marinade. Put into the refrigerator and leave for at least 2 hours. Soak the wooden skewers in enough water to cover for 30 minutes (to prevent burning).

3. For the yogurt sauce, peel and press the garlic. Put into a bowl with the rest of the sauce ingredients and mix thoroughly. Season with salt and pepper. Chill in the refrigerator.

4. Heat the broiler (grill). Take the meat out of the marinade and thread on the wooden skewers. Broil (grill) on all sides for 5–7 minutes. Meanwhile, fold the pita breads and briefly toast/warm them. Cut the lemon into 8 wedges.

5. Arrange the kebabs on plates with the pita bread. Garnish with salad and sprinkle with yogurt sauce. The remaining sauce can be served separately.

Lamb Patties in Pita Bread

Ingredients

1 small bread roll, stale

About 1 lb / 500 g ground lamb

½ small bunch (1 oz / 25 g) fresh mint leaves, finely chopped (reserve a few whole leaves for garnish)

1 egg

2 oz / 50 g feta cheese, crumbled

1 clove garlic, minced

Salt and freshly ground pepper, to taste

1 good pinch cumin

4 tbsp vegetable oil

2 beefsteak tomatoes

6 lettuce leaves, torn into bite-size pieces

6 pita breads, warmed in the oven, split to form pockets

½ red onion, sliced into rings

Method

Prep and cook time: 30 min

1. Place the bread in a large bowl and add enough water to cover; soak briefly, then squeeze out the water.

2. Discard the water in the bowl and add the lamb, soaked bread, chopped mint, egg, feta, garlic, salt, pepper and cumin; mix well to combine.

3. With moistened hands shape the ground meat mixture into six patties. Heat the oil in a skillet and fry the patties, turning once, until no longer pink inside, 6–10 minutes.

4. Meanwhile, slice the tomatoes in half and squeeze out the seeds; finely chop. Combine the lettuce with the reserved mint leaves. Line the pita pockets with half of the lettuce, onions and tomatoes.

5. Place the patties in the pita bread pockets and tuck the remaining lettuce and mint leaves around them. Season with salt and pepper and serve at once.

Lamb Biryani

Ingredients

1½ lb / 650 g lamb (leg)

1–2 onions

7 tbsp ghee or clarified butter

2 tsp freshly grated ginger

3 cloves garlic, pressed

6 cardamom pods

5 cloves

1 piece cinnamon stick (¾–1 inch / 2–3 cm)

½ tsp ground cumin

½ tsp turmeric

Chili powder, to taste

⅔ cup / 150 g yogurt

⅔ cup /150 ml meat broth (stock)

Salt

1½ cups / 300 g basmati rice

⅓ cup / 50 g raisins

4 tbsp milk

A few saffron threads

6 tbsp blanched almonds

Cilantro (coriander) leaves, to garnish

Method

Prep and cook time: 2 hours 15 min

1. Preheat the oven to 350°F (180°C / Gas Mark 4).

2. Cut the meat into bite-size pieces. Peel and finely dice the onions. Heat 4 tablespoons ghee (or clarified butter) in a pan and sauté half of the onions until translucent. Add the ginger, cardamom, garlic, cloves, cinnamon and meat and fry, stirring frequently, until the meat is lightly browned on all sides. Stir in the ground spices, yogurt and broth (stock) and season with salt. Cover and simmer over a low heat for 45–60 minutes, stirring occasionally (it will be very thick).

3. Sauté the rest of the onions in a pan without letting them color. Wash the rice in a sieve under running water and add to the onions with just double the amount of lightly salted water. Bring to a boil and cook, covered, over a very low heat for about 5 minutes.

4. Put the meat into a greased baking dish. Drain the rice and mix with the raisins. Heat the milk, add the saffron and 2 tablespoons ghee and let them dissolve. Add the milk to the rice and mix with the meat in the dish.

5. Put a lid on the dish (or seal with aluminum foil) and cook in the oven (middle shelf) for about 1 hour.

6. Lightly toast the almonds in the remaining ghee. Before serving fluff up the lamb biryani with a fork, season to taste and spoon onto plates.

7. Scatter some cilantro (coriander) over the top and serve.

Braised Pork
with Mushrooms and Olives

Ingredients

2¼ lbs / 1 kg pork loin

1 tbsp flour

2 cloves garlic

3 cups / 250 g small button mushrooms

4 tbsp olive oil

1 cups / 250 ml white wine

1¾ cups / 200 g green olives, pitted

Salt & freshly milled pepper

2 tbsp chopped parsley, to garnish

Method
Prep and cook time: 30 min

1. Wash the pork, then pat dry with paper towel and cut into cubes. Sprinkle flour all over the meat.

2. Peel and finely chop the garlic. Clean the mushrooms and cut into slices.

3. Fry the mushrooms in a skillet in 2 tablespoons hot oil, then remove and set aside.

4. Heat the remaining oil in the skillet, then fry the meat on all sides until browned. Add the garlic and pour in the white wine. Add the mushrooms and the olives, then season with salt and pepper.

5. Cover with a lid and simmer on a low heat for about 10–15 minutes. Add a little water if necessary.

6. Season to taste with salt and pepper, sprinkle chopped parsley over the top and serve.

Spicy Pork Ragout

Ingredients

1¾ lb / 800 g pork neck, cut into bite-size cubes

1 large white onion

3 cloves garlic

1 stick celery

1 carrot

14 oz / 500 g tomatoes, fresh or canned

4 tbsp olive oil

¾–1 cup / 200 ml red wine

1 tbsp tomato paste (purée)

1 tbsp finely chopped parsley

2 tsp sugar

Salt & freshly milled pepper

¾–1 cup / 200 ml vegetable broth (stock)

½ tsp cayenne pepper

1 tsp paprika

Fresh oregano, to garnish (optional)

Method
Prep and cook time: 2 hours 15 min

1. Peel and finely chop the onion and garlic. Wash the celery and peel the carrot. Chop both as finely as possible.

2. If using fresh tomatoes, drop them into boiling water for a few seconds, then immediately into cold water. Now skin the tomatoes, then quarter, de-seed and dice.

3. Heat the olive oil in a stew pot and quickly brown the meat on all sides. Take out and set aside.

4. Then in the same oil, sweat the onion, celery, carrot and garlic over a medium heat. Add the meat, sweat briefly with the vegetables, then pour in the red wine.

5. Cook until the wine has evaporated slightly, then stir in the tomatoes and tomato paste (purée). Add the parsley, season with salt and pepper and add the sugar.

6. Bring to a boil, then add the vegetable broth (stock) and simmer over a low heat for about 2 hours.

7. 15 minutes before the end of cooking time, stir in the cayenne pepper and paprika. Check the seasoning and add a little more salt and pepper to taste.

8. If the ragout becomes too dry while cooking, stir in 1–2 tablespoons of water. Garnish with oregano, if using.

Chorizo Stew
with Crème Fraîche

Ingredients

8 oz / 250 g chorizo (Spanish spiced pork sausage)

2 onions

1–2 garlic cloves

14 oz / 400 g potatoes

1 pack of soup vegetables (including, for example, leek, celery, parsnip, turnip) – about 1lb / 450 g

2 carrots

3 tbsp olive oil

1 can tomatoes (about 14 oz / 400 g)

2 cups / 500 ml vegetable broth (stock)

Salt & freshly milled pepper

1 bay leaf

1–2 tsp oregano, dried

1 1/3 cups / 200 g canned chickpeas, drained

A small tub of crème fraîche

Fresh parsley, to garnish

Method

Prep and cook time: 50 min

1. Peel the onions and the garlic. Cut the onions in half, then into small wedges. Chop the garlic. Peel the chorizo sausage and cut into slices.

2. Peel the potatoes and cut into cubes. Wash the soup vegetables and chop into small pieces. Peel the carrots and cut into rings.

3. Fry the chorizo sausage in a little oil in a flameproof casserole, then add the onions and the garlic and sauté until soft.

4. Add the potatoes, soup vegetables, carrots and tomatoes and pour in the vegetable broth (stock). Season with salt, pepper, bay leaf and oregano.

5. Cover and simmer gently for about 30 minutes on a low heat.

6. Rinse the chickpeas (garbanzo beans), then add to the stew and heat. Season with salt and pepper and serve with a spoonful of crème fraîche and fresh parsley.

Cassoulet with Knuckle of Pork

Ingredients

1 small knuckle of pork

1 1/2 cups / 300 g dried cannellini beans

2 onions

2 cloves

1 bay leaf

2 garlic cloves

2 carrots

4 scallions (spring onions)

2 sprigs rosemary

1/2 cup / 100 g black olives, pitted

Salt & freshly milled pepper

Method

Prep and cook time: 2 hours plus 12 hours soaking time

1. Soak the beans overnight. Drain the beans.

2. Peel one onion and press the cloves and the bay leaf into it.

3. Put the onion together with the beans and the pork in a large pan, cover with water and simmer for about 1 1/2 hours. Add water if needed and remove any scum.

4. In the meantime, peel the garlic, carrots and remaining onion and roughly chop. Wash and trim the scallions (spring onions) and cut into pieces.

5. About 30 minutes before the end of cooking time, put the vegetables, the rosemary and the olives into the pan.

6. At the end of cooking time (when the beans are cooked), take the pork out of the pan, remove the bone and cut the meat into cubes. Remove the onion with the garlic clove.

7. Put the pork back into the pan and season to taste with salt and pepper.

Pot-au-Feu
with Belly Pork

Ingredients

3 lb 4 oz / 1½ kg pork belly, with thin layer of fat but no skin

Salt & freshly milled pepper

6 fresh sage leaves

2 tbsp sunflower oil

2 stalks celery

2 leeks

6 cloves garlic

3 carrots

4 large potatoes, boiling

½ small savoy cabbage

2 bay leaves

6 sprigs thyme

2 sprigs sage

1 sprig rosemary

1 sprig marjoram

4 shallots

1 handful of parsley leaves, chopped

Method

Prep and cook time: 3 hours

1. Season the meat with salt and pepper, place the sage leaves on the top and roll up tight. Fasten with kitchen twine.

2. Fry the meat in hot oil on all sides. Place in a large pan and pour in about 15 cups (3 liters) water. Add 1 teaspoon salt and bring to a boil. Simmer for 1 hour, scooping off any scum.

3. In the meantime wash and trim the vegetables and tie the herbs together. Chop the celery and the leek into 3-inch (7-cm) pieces. Peel and chop the garlic.

4. Peel the carrots, cut in half lengthways, then into quarters. Peel the potatoes and roughly chop. Cut the savoy cabbage into 4–6 wedges.

5. At the end of cooking time, add the carrots, the herb bouquet and the garlic and simmer for another 30 minutes.

6. Now add the rest of the ingredients, apart from the parsley, and simmer for 1 hour.

7. Take the meat out of the soup and remove the kitchen twine. Cut into slices and place into bowls. Spoon some of the soup and vegetables over the top, garnish with parsley and serve.

Toad in the Hole
(Sausages in Batter)

Ingredients

6–10 fresh pork sausages

1 cup / 125 g flour

½ tsp baking powder

½ tsp salt

2 large eggs

1¼ cups / 300 ml milk

3 tbsp / 40 g lard or oil

2 tbsp finely chopped parsley

Method

Prep and cook time: 1 hour plus standing time: 20 min

1. Preheat the oven to 400°F (200°C / Gas Mark 6). For the Yorkshire pudding batter, put the flour, baking powder and salt into a mixing bowl. Add the eggs and milk and mix well. Leave to stand for 20 minutes.

2. Put the lard (or oil) into a roasting dish and put into the oven. Prick the sausages several times, put into the hot fat and roast in the oven until lightly browned.

3. Take the sausages out of the dish, pour in the batter and lay the sausages in the batter. Sprinkle with parsley and bake in the oven for 30–40 minutes.

4. The Yorkshire pudding should be light, crisp and well risen.

Pork Ribs with Chilies

Ingredients

3 lbs / 1.5 kg pork ribs (ask your butcher to chop into separate ribs)

2 oranges

3 tbsp soy sauce

2 tbsp tomato paste (purée)

2 tbsp sunflower oil

2 tbsp honey

1 inch / 3 cm fresh ginger, peeled and grated

6 mild red chili peppers, slit open length wise and de-seeded

4 scallions (spring onions), green parts only, chopped into 1½-inch / 5-cm long strips

Method

Prep and cook time: 1 hour 20 min plus 2 hours marinading

1. Place the ribs in boiling water and simmer for around 45 minutes.

2. Zest and juice the oranges. Mix the zest and juice with the soy sauce, tomato paste (purée), oil, honey and ginger.

3. Remove the ribs from the water and drain. Whilst still hot pour over the marinade mixture, cover and allow to marinade for at least 2 hours in the fridge.

4. Preheat the broiler (grill) and lay the ribs on a baking tray. Drizzle with marinade and broil for around 10 minutes until slightly crunchy.

5. Turn the ribs, sprinkle with the chili peppers and scallions and continue broiling for a further 5–10 minutes.

Pork Chops with Apples

Ingredients

3 tbsp vegetable oil, divided

4 pork chops

½ tsp curry powder

½ tsp honey

Salt and freshly ground pepper, to taste

2 apples, quartered and cut into
bite-size chunks

2 red onions, sliced

2 tbsp pine nuts

1 tbsp freshly chopped basil leaves,
to garnish

Method

Prep and cook time: 25 min

1. Preheat the oven to 250°F (130°C/ Gas Mark ½).

2. Heat 1 tablespoon of the oil in a nonstick skillet (frying pan) and sauté the chops on both sides until brown. Transfer to a baking dish.

3. In a small bowl, mix the curry powder with the honey and 1-2 tablespoons water. Brush the meat with the mixture and season with salt and pepper. Bake for 15–20 minutes, until the meat is just cooked in the center.

4. Meanwhile, add the remaining oil to the skillet, then add the apples, onions and pine nuts and fry all together for 2–3 minutes. Season with salt and pepper.

5. Put the chops on warmed plates, add a little of the apple and onion to each and serve scattered with basil.

Pork Chops with Mushrooms

Ingredients

1–2 tbsp all-purpose (plain) flour

4 boneless pork chops

2 tbsp vegetable oil

For the mushroom sauce:

2 tbsp butter

1 (10-oz) package / 300 g button mushrooms, quartered

1 onion, finely chopped

1 tbsp all-purpose (plain) flour

Scant 1 cup / 200 ml light cream

Salt and freshly ground pepper, to taste

2 tbsp coarse-grained French mustard

1–2 tablespoons milk, as needed

For the vegetables:

Scant 1 cup / 200 ml vegetable broth (stock)

1 lb / 400 g carrots, peeled and cut into matchstick-size pieces

1 cup / 100 g sugarsnap peas, trimmed and halved

Method

Prep and cook time: 25 min

1. Spread the flour on a plate. Coat the chops with the flour, shaking off the excess. Heat the oil in a skillet, add the chops and cook until browned and just cooked in the center. Remove from heat and set aside, keeping warm.

2. To prepare the sauce, heat the butter in a skillet; add mushrooms and onion and sauté until soft. Sprinkle with the flour and sauté for 1 minute. Pour in the cream, stirring constantly, and bring to a boil. Season to taste with salt, pepper and mustard. Add milk as needed to thin the sauce. Place the pork chops in the sauce and keep warm over low heat.

3. Meanwhile, bring the vegetable broth (stock) to a boil in a saucepan; add the carrots and simmer, covered, for about 5 minutes. Add the sugarsnap peas and simmer 1 minute; drain.

4. Place the pork chops onto plates, spooning mushroom sauce over the top. Serve with the vegetables.

Pork Escalope
with Mozzarella

Ingredients

2 large tomatoes

1 tbsp pitted green olives

1 tbsp pitted black olives

10 oz / 300 g mozzarella cheese

4 pork cutlets

5 tbsp olive oil

2 tbsp butter

4 tbsp basil pesto

Pepper

Basil leaves, for garnishing

Method

Prep and cook time: 45 min

1. Preheat the oven to 400°F (200° C /Gas Mark 6).

2. Slice the tomatoes and olives.

3. Drain and slice the mozzarella.

4. Put the cutlets between 2 pieces of plastic wrap and flatten slightly with a mallet or rolling pin.

5. Heat 1 tbsp oil and the butter in a large skillet and sear the cutlets quickly for 30 seconds each side.

6. Grease an ovenproof dish with the remaining olive oil.

7. Put the cutlets in the dish. Spread 1 tbsp of pesto on each of the cutlets, sprinkle the sliced olives on top and then add the mozzarella. Sprinkle with a little pepper.

8. Bake for 10–15 minutes. Garnish with the basil leaves and serve.

Caribbean Style Pork

Ingredients

8 ripe tomatoes

½ ripe mango, pitted and finely chopped

3 tbsp mango juice

2 tbsp snipped chives

6 tbsp olive oil, divided

Hot red pepper sauce, to taste

Salt and freshly ground pepper, to taste

2 tbsp finely chopped basil leaves

1 tbsp finely chopped rosemary leaves

1 tbsp tomato paste (purée)

3 cloves garlic, finely chopped

4 (6-oz / 180 g) boneless pork chops

Method

Prep and cook time: 30 min

1. Fill a large bowl with ice water. Bring a large saucepan of water to a boil. One or two at a time, add the tomatoes and cook 8–10 seconds; quickly remove them with a slotted spoon to the ice water to cool. Repeat with the remaining tomatoes. Drain the tomatoes and slip off the skins. Halve and squeeze out the seeds; finely chop.

2. Combine the chopped tomatoes with the mango, mango juice, snipped chives, 2 tablespoons of the oil, hot pepper sauce, salt and plenty of pepper; set aside.

3. Preheat the broiler (grill) to medium high. Heat the remaining 4 tablespoons oil in a skillet over medium heat; add the basil, rosemary, tomato paste (purée) and garlic. Cook, stirring, for 1 minute. Add the chops and turn once or twice so that both sides are coated in the tomato-herb mixture. Place the skillet under the broiler. Cook, turning frequently, until juices run barely pink when pierced with a fork, about 10 minutes. Season with salt and plenty of pepper and serve at once with the tomato and mango sauce.

Spicy Pork Vindaloo

Ingredients

1 lb 12 oz / 800 g pork (e. g. shoulder)

2 onions

2 cloves garlic

1 tbsp mustard oil

1 tsp ginger, freshly grated

½ tsp cumin

1 tsp mustard seeds

½ tsp curcuma (turmeric)

1 stick cinnamon

1 tsp tamarind paste

1 tsp brown sugar

1 lemon, juice

1 new potato

Oil, for frying

Method

Prep and cook time: 1 hour

1. Wash the pork, pat dry, then dice.

2. Peel and finely chop the onions and the garlic.

3. Fry the meat in the hot mustard oil. Add the onions, garlic and the spices and sauté. Pour in the lemon juice, stir in the tamarind paste and sugar and add about 2/3 cup (150 ml) water. Cover and simmer gently over a low heat for 45–50 minutes. Add a little water if needed.

4. For the garnish, slice the potato into very thin sticks and fry in hot oil until golden brown. Drain on a paper towel and lightly salt.

5. Season the curry, garnish with the potato sticks and serve.

Pork Curry with Tamarind

Ingredients

2 oz / 50 g pressed tamarinds

2 onions

1 lb 6 oz / 600 g pork

2 tbsp fish sauce

2 tbsp oil

1¾ cups / 400 ml unsweetened coconut milk

2 tbsp yellow curry paste

Salt

Sugar

½ bunch Thai basil

Method

Prep and cook time: 1 hour

1. Soak the tamarinds in ½ cup / 125 ml water for about 30 minutes. Peel and finely slice the onions.

2. Cut the meat into bite-size cubes. Put the meat into a bowl with the fish sauce and let stand for 10 minutes.

3. Put the oil in a large skillet (frying pan) and brown the meat on all sides in batches.

4. Take the creamy top of the coconut milk and put into a saucepan. Add the rest of the coconut milk to the skillet with the meat, cover and simmer for about 20 minutes.

5. Bring the coconut cream to a boil in the saucepan and simmer for 2 minutes. Add the curry paste and stir until dissolved. Add the onions and cook for about 1 minute. Transfer the meat and coconut sauce from the skillet to the saucepan.

6. Squeeze out the tamarind, discard the fibers and add the liquid to the curry. Simmer for about 15 minutes, until the meat is cooked. Add salt and sugar to taste. Garnish with Thai basil and serve.

Pork Curry
with Fresh Herbs

Ingredients

1½ lb / 700 g lean pork (without skin or bones)

1 onion

1 dried chili

3 tbsp oil

2 tsp finely grated fresh ginger

A good pinch of ground coriander

½ tsp ground curcuma (turmeric)

A good pinch of ground cumin

A pinch of ground cloves

2 tbsp dark soy sauce

Salt & freshly milled pepper

1 tbsp chopped parsley

Scallion (spring onion) greens, cut into rings

Method

Prep and cook time: 1 hour 15 min

1. Wash the meat, pat dry and roughly dice. Peel and dice the onion. Chop the dried chili.

2. Heat the oil and quickly brown the meat on all sides. Season with salt and pepper and add the onion, ginger and chili. Fry gently for about 3 minutes. Then stir in the coriander, curcuma (turmeric), cumin and cloves, and add ¾–1 cup / 200 ml water and the soy sauce. Cover and cook for about 45 minutes.

3. Serve sprinkled with parsley and scallion (spring onion) rings.

Sweet and Sour Pork

Ingredients

1 lb / 450 g pork fillet, cut into cubes

1 tbsp rice wine

1 tbsp light soy sauce

2 tsp sesame oil

1 egg, lightly beaten

4 tbsp cornstarch (cornflour)

Oil for deep frying

For the sauce:

1 large carrot, sliced diagonally

2/3 cup / 150 ml chicken broth (stock)

1 tbsp light soy sauce

2 tsp dark soy sauce

2 tsp sesame oil

4 tsp rice vinegar

1 tbsp sugar

2 tbsp tomato catsup (ketchup)

2 tsp cornstarch (cornflour)

1 red bell pepper, de-seeded and chopped into diamonds

4 scallions (spring onions), trimmed and roughly chopped

cilantro (fresh coriander) leaves, to garnish

Method

Prep and cook time: 40 min

1. Put the pork into a bowl with rice wine, soy sauce and sesame oil and marinate for 15 minutes.

2. Mix together 1 tbsp cornstarch with the egg.

3. Heat the oil in a deep-fat fryer to 180°C/350°F.

4. Put the rest of the cornstarch onto a plate. Lift the pork from the marinade and toss in the cornstarch to dust. Then dip the pork into the egg and cornstarch mixture to coat.

5. Deep fry the pork for about 5 minutes, until golden, cooking in batches.

6. Drain the pork on paper towels and keep warm.

7. For the sauce blanch the carrots in boiling water for 2 minutes to soften, then drain.

8. Put the chicken broth, light and dark soy sauce, sesame oil, rice vinegar, sugar, catsup (ketchup) and cornstarch mixture into a pan and bring to a boil.

9. Add the carrots, pepper and scallions (spring onions).

10. Add the fried pork balls and serve garnished with cilantro (coriander) leaves.

Pork in Plum Sauce

Ingredients

2 lbs / 800 g pork fillet, cut into strips

2 tbsp sesame oil

2 carrots, peeled and chopped into thin strips

1 clove garlic, peeled and finely chopped

1 inch / 3 cm ginger, peeled and grated

Soy sauce

2–3 tbsp plum sauce

1 scallion (spring onion), chopped into thin rings

Method

Prep and cook time: 25 min

1. Heat the oil in a wok or large skillet until very hot, add the meat and seal on all sides.

2. Add the carrot, garlic, ginger, a little water and 2 tbsp soy sauce.

3. Stir in the plum sauce and simmer for 3–4 minutes stirring occasionally.

4. Season the meat with soy sauce and serve scattered with scallion rings and garnished with parsley.

Stir Fried Pork and Vegetables
with Egg-Fried Rice

Ingredients

1 tbsp sesame oil

1-inch / 3-cm piece fresh ginger
root, grated

1 clove garlic, minced

1 red onion, sliced

1 lb / 450 g lean pork, cut into strips

1 red bell pepper, coarsely chopped

1 yellow bell pepper, coarsely chopped

¼ lb / 100 g chestnut or brown button
mushrooms, quartered

2 tbsp sweet chili sauce

2 tbsp dark soy sauce

2 tbsp teriyaki sauce

½ lb / 200 g snow peas or
sugarsnap peas

Method
Prep and cook time: 30 min

1. Heat the sesame oil in a large wok or skillet; add the ginger, garlic and onion and stir-fry for 2 minutes.

2. Add the pork and fry for 5 minutes, turning as needed, until browned. Add the red and yellow peppers and the mushrooms into the wok and cook, stirring, for another 5 minutes.

3. Pour in the sweet chili sauce, soy sauce and teriyaki sauce, then add the snow peas or sugar snaps. Cook for a further 2–3 minutes; set aside and keep warm.

4. For the fried rice, beat together the egg and sesame oil in a small bowl and set aside.

5. Heat the vegetable oil in a clean wok or skillet, then add the rice and stir-fry for about 3–4 minutes.

6. Add the peas and scallions (spring onions) and stir-fry for about 3 minutes. Season with salt and pepper and splash in the soy sauce, then push to one side of the wok.

7. Pour the beaten egg mixture into the other side of the wok and leave for about 10 seconds so it begins to set. Using a chopstick, briskly swirl around the egg to break it up, then toss it gently with the rice. Stir-fry for a further minute and serve at once with the pork and vegetables.

Meatballs with Gnocci and Tomatoes

Ingredients

½ lb / 225g ground (minced) pork

½ lb / 225g ground (minced) beef

1 egg, beaten

1 onion, finely chopped

¼ cup / 50 g plain dry breadcrumbs

1 tsp oregano

1 tbsp olive oil

2 cloves garlic, crushed

11 oz / 300 g gnocchi

12 cherry tomatoes

8 oz / 250 g mascarpone

1/3 cup / 100 ml milk

Salt and freshly ground pepper, to taste

¼ cup / 225g grated cheddar cheese

To garnish:

1 tbsp chopped chives

Method

Prep and cook time: 1 hour

1. Heat the oven to 400° F (200° C / Gas Mark 6). Using your hands, combine pork, beef, egg, onion, breadcrumbs and oregano in a large bowl, then shape into 12 meatballs.

2. Heat the oil in a large skillet and add the meatballs and garlic. Fry for 10 minutes, turning occasionally, until browned all over.

3. Bring a large pan of salted water to a boil. Add the gnocchi, return to the boil and cook for 3 minutes. Drain.

4. Tip the meatballs and garlic into a large shallow baking dish and add the gnocchi and cherry tomatoes.

5. Gently warm the mascarpone in a saucepan with the milk, stirring until smooth. Season to taste with salt and pepper.

6. Pour the mascarpone mixture over the meatballs, gnocchi and tomatoes. Sprinkle evenly with the cheddar cheese. Bake for 20 minutes until thoroughly warmed through. Garnish with chopped chives to serve.

Egg and Bacon Pie

Ingredients

12 oz (about 300 g) puff pastry, thawed if frozen

18-oz container / 200 g sour cream

¼ lb / 125 g bacon, diced

½ bunch parsley, finely chopped

Hot paprika, to taste

Salt and freshly ground pepper, to taste

4 eggs

Method

Prep and cook time: 40 min

1. Preheat the oven to 400° F (200°C / Gas Mark 6). Grease a 12-inch (30-cm) tart pan.

2. Roll out the pastry into a circle slightly bigger than the tart pan. Line the pan with the pastry, trimming off the excess. Cut out a few decorative shapes from the pastry trimmings. Brush the edge of the pastry with water and decorate with the cut-out shapes, pressing on lightly.

3. Mix the sour cream with the diced bacon, parsley, paprika, salt and pepper; spread onto the pastry, making 4 indentations with a spoon. Carefully break the eggs into the indentations. Bake about 20 minutes, until the eggs are set. Serve immediately.

Penne with Bacon, Walnuts and Gorgonzola

Ingredients

14 oz / 400 g penne pasta

1 onion, finely chopped

2 tbsp nut oil

4 oz / 100 g diced bacon

½ cup / 50 g shelled walnuts

Some fresh parsley

Salt & freshly milled pepper

4 oz / 100 g Gorgonzola cheese (or other blue cheese)

Method

Prep and cook time: 25 min

1. Cook the pasta in boiling, salted water until al dente, then refresh in cold water and drain.

2. Heat the oil and fry the onion and bacon until golden brown. Add the walnuts, fry briefly, then add the pasta and fry briefly. Shred the parsley leaves. Add to the pasta and season with pepper and a little salt.

3. Crumble the Gorgonzola (or other blue cheese, such as Roquefort) over the pasta and serve at once on plates or in bowls.

Pasta Ham Bake

Ingredients

2 eggs

1 cup / 250 ml whipping cream

2 tbsp crème fraîche

Scant ½ cup / 50 g grated Cheddar cheese

Salt and freshly milled pepper

Pinch nutmeg

8 oz / 250 g cooked ham, diced

14 oz / 400 g ribbon pasta

1 tbsp soft butter

2 tbsp breadcrumbs

2 tbsp chopped fresh chives, to garnish

Method

Prep and cook time: 1 hour

1. Separate the eggs. Mix the cream and the crème fraîche with the egg yolks until smooth.

2. Stir in the grated cheese and season with salt, pepper and nutmeg. Add the diced ham and mix well with the ribbon pasta. Whisk the egg whites until stiff, and then fold into the pasta.

3. Preheat the oven to 400°F (200°C / Gas Mark 6). Butter a baking dish and coat the base with breadcrumbs. Put the ribbon pasta mix in the dish and place in the oven for about 30 minutes until golden brown.

4. Sprinkle the chopped chives over the top and serve.

Macaroni and Cheese with Ham

Ingredients

9 oz / 250 g macaroni

2 oz / 4 tbsp / 50 g butter

½ cup / 50 g all-purpose (plain) flour

4 cups / 900 ml milk

8 oz / 225 g Emmental cheese, grated

4 oz / 100 g wafer-thin ham slices, chopped

½ tsp freshly grated nutmeg

Method

Prep and cook time: 25 min

1. Heat the broiler (grill). Bring a large pot of salted water to a boil and add the pasta. Cook according to the package instructions, until al dente.

2. Meanwhile, melt the butter in a medium nonstick skillet. Add the flour and cook, stirring, for 1 minute. Gradually add the milk, whisking all the time to make a smooth sauce. Keep stirring until the sauce is thickened.

3. Drain the macaroni and add to the sauce with the cheese, ham and nutmeg.

4. Pour into an ovenproof dish and broil (grill) for 2–3 minutes, just until top is browned, then serve.

Pasta with Leek, Bacon and Herbs

Ingredients

14 oz / 400 g penne

4 slices (rashers) bacon

1 leek

2 cloves garlic

1 tbsp / 25 g butter

Scant ¾ cup / 60 g Parmesan cheese

Freshly milled pepper

Basil, shredded

Method

Prep and cook time: 30 min

1. Cook the pasta in plenty of boiling, salted water until al dente.

2. Cut the bacon into thin strips. Trim and wash the leek and cut the white and light green parts into thin rings. Peel the garlic. Heat the butter in a pan, add the bacon and fry briefly. Add the leek rings and press the garlic into the pan. Sauté briefly.

3. Mix the pasta with the bacon and leeks. Season with pepper. Serve sprinkled with Parmesan cheese shavings and shredded basil.

Spaghetti with Bacon, Feta and Chili

Ingredients

14 oz / 400 g spaghetti

4 thin slices (rashers) bacon

5 oz / 150 g feta cheese

1 red chili

2 oz / 4 tbsp / 50 g butter

2 tbsp fresh basil leaves, finely chopped

1 tsp lime zest

Salt & freshly milled pepper

Method

Prep and cook time: 20 min

1. Cook the spaghetti in boiling, salted water until al dente, catching about ½ a cup (125 ml) of cooking water when draining.

2. In the meantime cut the bacon into strips and dice the feta cheese. Wash the chili, de-seed, then finely chop.

3. Melt the butter in a skillet and fry the bacon. Add the chopped chili, then remove from the heat.

4. Toss the spaghetti in the bacon and the reserved cooking water, and carefully mix in the feta cheese, basil and lime zest. Season with salt and pepper and serve immediately.

Spaghetti Carbonara

Ingredients

14 oz / 400 g spaghetti

4 slices fatty (streaky) bacon

2 tbsp oil

3 eggs

3 tbsp light cream (single cream)

Generous 1 cup / 100 g freshly grated Parmesan cheese

Some chives, chopped

2 cloves garlic

Salt & freshly milled pepper

Method

Prep and cook time: 25 min

1. Cut the bacon into thin strips. Fry the bacon gently in the oil in a large pan.

2. Cook the spaghetti in boiling, salted water according to the instructions on the packet until al dente.

3. Whisk the eggs and cream and season with salt and pepper. Stir in half of the Parmesan cheese and the chives.

4. Remove the crispy bacon slices from the pan and keep warm. Peel the garlic, finely chop and gently sauté in the bacon fat.

5. Drain the spaghetti well, then place immediately in the pan and toss in the bacon fat. Now take the pan from the heat. Pour in the egg–cream mixture and stir until the spaghetti is coated with the sauce. Mix in the bacon, season with freshly milled pepper, sprinkle the remaining Parmesan cheese over the top and serve.

Risotto
with Zucchini, Ham and Parmesan

Ingredients

4 oz / 1 stick / 100 g butter

1 onion, finely chopped

1²/₃ cups / 350 g risotto rice

½ cup / 125 ml dry white wine

4 cups / 1 liter beef or chicken broth (stock), hot

2 zucchini (courgettes), trimmed and thinly sliced

4 scallions (spring onions), coarsely chopped

4 tbsp olive oil

¾ cup / 100 g grated Parmesan cheese, divided

1 cup / 150 g chopped air-dried ham

½ bunch basil

Salt & pepper, to taste

Method

Prep and cook time: 30 min

1. Melt half of the butter in a skillet and sauté the onion until soft. Add the rice and stir over the heat until the grains are translucent, about 5 minutes.

2. Stir in the wine and cook until it has evaporated. Then gradually add the hot broth (stock) ½ cup at a time, stirring and adding the next ½ cup when the last addition has been absorbed, until the rice is almost cooked (about 15 minutes).

3. Meanwhile, heat the oil in a skillet and sauté the zucchini (courgettes) and scallions (spring onions) until softened, 3–5 minutes. Set aside.

4. Stir ½ cup of the Parmesan into the risotto and cook, stirring, 5 minutes more, adding a little more broth if necessary. Stir in the rest of the butter, the ham and vegetables into the risotto and season with salt and pepper.

5. Shred half of the basil leaves and stir into the risotto. Spoon the risotto onto plates and garnish with the remaining basil leaves. Top with the remaining Parmesan cheese and serve.

Pot au Feu

Ingredients

1 chicken, weighing about 2½ lbs / 1.2 kg, cut into 8 pieces

3 tbsp olive oil

1 tbsp thyme, dried

2 bay leaves

1 clove garlic, finely diced

1 bunch scallions (spring onions), trimmed and chopped

7 oz / 200 g small carrots, washed

14 oz / 400 g small potatoes, scrubbed

8 oz / 250 g green asparagus, trimmed and cut into small pieces

Chicken broth (stock) granules or cube

Salt & freshly milled pepper

Method

Prep and cook time: 1 hour

1. Season the chicken pieces well and fry on all sides in a little oil until browned.

2. Add the thyme, bay leaves and garlic. Sweat briefly with the chicken, then add sufficient cold water to cover the contents of the pan.

3. Simmer gently for 30 minutes, removing the scum from time to time.

4. Add the prepared vegetables except the asparagus and simmer for a further 15 minutes. Add the asparagus and simmer for 5 more minutes.

5. Add the broth (stock) granules and season with salt and pepper to taste.

Chicken Stew
with Chanterelles

Ingredients

1 chicken, jointed (legs, wings, breast)

2 large scallions (spring onions)

14 oz / 400 g baking potatoes

2 carrots

2 parsnips

Salt & freshly milled pepper

2 tbsp olive oil

2 cloves garlic, peeled

1¼ cups / 300 ml chicken broth (stock)

1 bay leaf

7 oz / 200 g chanterelles

2 tbsp / 25 g butter

2 tbsp thyme leaves

A few fresh sage leaves

Method

Prep and cook time: 1 h 15 min

1. Wash and trim the scallions (spring onions) and cut into 2-inch (5-cm) lengths.

2. Peel the potatoes and dice finely, so that they will disintegrate and thicken the sauce.

3. Peel the carrots and parsnips and quarter lengthways.

4. Season the chicken pieces with salt and pepper, heat the oil in a large pan and brown the chicken pieces on all sides. Then add the vegetables, garlic and the broth (stock).

5. Add the bay leaf, cover and stew gently for about 1 hour. Stir frequently and add more broth if necessary.

6. Clean the chanterelles and sauté in butter. Remove from the heat.

7. 5 minutes before the end of cooking time add the herbs and chanterelles to the stew. Check the seasoning of the sauce and serve.

Spicy Poussin

Ingredients

4 poussins, each weighing about 1 lb/ 450 g or 2 spring chickens

Sea salt

4 garlic cloves

1 tbsp dried oregano

2 tsp paprika

1 tsp coarsely ground black pepper

Grated zest and juice 2 lemons

4 tbsp olive oil

1¼ cups / 300 ml chicken broth (stock)

2 tbsp balsamic vinegar

2 roasted red bell peppers

4 handfuls wild arugula (rocket)

2 oz / 50 g Parmesan cheese

8 tsp chili jam, to garnish

Method

Prep and cook time: 1 hour 25 min

1. Preheat the oven to 400°F (200°C / Gas Mark 6). Put the poussins in a large roasting pan and season with sea salt.

2. Crush the garlic and sprinkle over the poussins with the oregano, paprika, black pepper and lemon zest. Drizzle over the lemon juice and olive oil.

3. Add the chicken stock and balsamic vinegar to the roasting pan, cover with foil and roast for 20 minutes or 35 minutes for spring chicken.

4. Remove the foil, baste the birds with the juices and roast for a further 15 minutes until the birds are browned and cooked through.

5. Meanwhile, cut the red peppers into quarters, discarding the cores and seeds.

6. Place the poussins on serving plates with some of the pan juices, each with 2 pepper quarters and a handful of arugula (rocket).

7. Using a vegetable peeler, shave the Parmesan cheese on top. Season with black pepper and serve garnished with chili jam.

Roast Lemon Chicken

Ingredients

3 lemons

2 tbsp vegetable oil

Salt and pepper

1 large chicken

2 lb / 900 g small waxy potatoes

8 sprigs thyme

2 cups / 475 ml chicken broth (stock)

4 scallions (spring onions)

1 red bell pepper

1 tbsp honey

4 tsp sherry

Method

Prep and cook time: 1 hour 30 min

1. Preheat the oven to 375°F (190°C / Gas Mark 5). Remove the zest from 1 lemon and slice all the lemons.

2. Mix half the lemon zest with 1 tbsp oil and salt and pepper. Rub the mixture all over the chicken. Tie the legs together with string and tuck the wings under the chicken.

3. Peel the potatoes and put in a roasting pan with the lemon slices. Place the chicken, breast side down, in the pan and add the thyme.

4. Roast in the oven for 30 minutes, occasionally pouring some of the chicken stock over the top and basting with the pan juices.

5. Meanwhile, cut the scallions (spring onions) into short lengths. Roughly chop the red pepper, discarding the core and seeds.

6. Remove the chicken from the pan and add the scallions and red pepper to the roasting pan.

7. Put the honey, sherry, remaining oil and lemon zest in a bowl and mix together. Return the chicken to the pan, breast side up, baste with the marinade and sprinkle with salt and pepper.

8. Roast the chicken for a further 35–45 minutes until golden brown and thoroughly cooked.

Chicken with Lemon and Thyme

Ingredients

1 chicken, about 2½ lb / 1.2 kg

10 sprigs thyme, plus a few for garnish

3 tbsp olive oil

1 cup / 250 ml white wine

4 lemons

Salt and freshly ground pepper

Method

Prep and cook time: 1 hour

1. Preheat the oven to 375°F (180°C / Gas Mark 5).

2. Rinse the chicken and dry well. Divide into eight pieces.

3. Strip the leaves from the thyme sprigs. Put the leaves between the skin and the meat. Season with salt and pepper.

4. Heat the oil in a roasting pan and brown the chicken on all sides. Pour in the white wine.

5. Quarter the lemons and add them to the pan along with the remaining thyme sprigs.

6. Roast for about 30 minutes, basting occasionally.

Pan Cooked Chicken
with Rice and Veg

Ingredients

7 oz / 1 cup / 200 g long grain rice

3½ cups / 900 ml vegetable broth (stock)

4 chicken legs, with skin on

Salt

2 green bell peppers

4 tomatoes

2¾ cups / 400 g frozen peas

2 tbsp paprika

1–2 tsp cayenne pepper

Method

Prep and cook time: 1 hour

1. Preheat the oven to 325°F (170°C / Gas Mark 3).

2. Wash and drain the rice. Put into a saucepan with 2½ cups (600 ml) of the vegetable broth (stock), bring to the boil and simmer for about 20 minutes until tender. Drain.

3. Season the chicken legs with salt, put into an ovenproof dish, and add the remaining vegetable stock. Cook the chicken in the oven for 20 minutes.

4. Meanwhile, roughly dice the green peppers, discarding the cores and seeds. Cut the tomatoes in half and dice the flesh, discarding the seeds. Add the peas, peppers and tomatoes to the rice and season with salt.

5. Remove the chicken legs from the baking dish. Put the rice and vegetables into the dish and mix with the meat juices. Place the chicken legs on top of the rice and sprinkle with paprika and cayenne pepper.

6. Return to the oven and cook for a further 15 minutes until the chicken legs are golden brown.

Garlic Chicken

Ingredients

1 red onion

40 garlic cloves

1 lemon

4 chicken breasts, on the bone and skinned

Salt and pepper

5 tbsp olive oil

6 sprigs thyme

4 bay leaves

½ cup / 125 ml water

Method

Prep and cook time: 1 hour 50 min

1. Preheat the oven to 400°F (200°C / Gas Mark 6). Cut the onion into wedges and skin the garlic cloves. Slice the lemon.

2. Generously season the chicken with salt and pepper.

3. Heat the oil in a large flameproof casserole. Add the chicken and onion and cook for 10 minutes, turning occasionally, until the chicken is browned all on all sides.

4. Add the thyme, 2 bay leaves, lemon slices and garlic cloves, baste with the oil and meat juices and pour in the water.

5. Cover with a tight fitting lid and cook in the oven for 1½ hours until the chicken and garlic are very tender. Serve garnished with the remaining bay leaves.

Creamy Chicken and Leeks

Ingredients

1 onion

4 baby leeks

2 tbsp olive oil

4 boneless chicken breasts, skinned

Salt and pepper

1 tbsp all-purpose (plain) flour

1¼ cups / 300 ml chicken stock

²/₃ cup / 200 ml crème fraîche

2 tbsp chopped fresh tarragon

1 cup / 200 g long-grain rice

Lime wedges, to garnish

Method

Prep and cook time: 40 min

1. Chop the onion. Cut the leeks into shreds. Cut the chicken into thick slices.

2. Heat the oil in a large skillet (frying pan) and add the onion and leeks. Cook gently for 2 minutes, then remove 1 tbsp of the lightly cooked leeks and set aside to garnish.

3. Add the chicken to the pan, season generously with salt and pepper and cook for 5 minutes until browned on all sides.

4. Sprinkle over the flour and cook for 1 minute, then gradually stir in the stock. Cover the pan and simmer for 15 minutes.

5. Cook the rice according to the packet instructions. Drain well.

6. Stir the crème fraîche and tarragon into the chicken and heat through for 2–3 minutes. Serve the chicken on top of the rice and garnish with the reserved leeks and a lime wedge.

Chicken and Ham Pie

Ingredients

1 lb / 450 g boneless chicken breasts, skinned

1¼ cups / 300 ml chicken broth (stock)

8 oz / 225 g cooked ham

1 shallot

2 oz / 4tbsp / 50 g butter

2 tbsp all-purpose (plain) flour

5 oz / 150 g crème fraîche

2 tbsp of lemon juice

2 egg yolks

3 tbsp grated Cheddar cheese

2 tbsp finely chopped fresh parsley

Freshly grated nutmeg

Salt and pepper

For the pastry:

2 cups / 200 g all-purpose (plain) flour

1 tsp salt

2½ oz / 5 tbsp / 70 g cold butter

2½ oz / 5 tbsp / 70 g shortening or lard

1–2 tbsp ice-cold water

Flour, for dusting

Method

Prep and cook time: 1 hour 30 min

1. To make the pastry, put the flour and salt into a large bowl. Add the butter and shortening or lard, in small pieces, and rub in with your fingertips until the mixture forms breadcrumbs. Add enough ice-cold water to form a dough. Wrap in plastic wrap (clingfilm) and put into the refrigerator while you make the filling.

2. Preheat the oven to 400°F (200°C / Gas Mark 6). Cut the chicken into small, bite-sized cubes. Put the stock into a saucepan and bring to the boil. Add the chicken and cook for 4–5 minutes. Remove from the pan with a slotted spoon, reserving the stock.

3. Cut the ham into small cubes, discarding any fat. Finely chop the shallot. Melt ½ oz (1 tbsp /15 g) butter in a saucepan. Add the shallot and fry until translucent. Add the ham and fry for about 3 minutes then remove from the heat.

4. Heat remaining butter in a separate pan. Add the flour and stir until it has absorbed the fat. Gradually stir in the broth (stock), bring to the boil, stirring, and then remove from the heat.

5. Put the crème fraîche, lemon juice and 1 egg yolk in a bowl and mix together. Stir into the sauce with the cheese. Add the chicken, ham and parsley and mix well together. Season with nutmeg, salt and pepper.

6. Divide the pastry in half and roll out each half on a floured surface into a round large enough to fit a 9-inch (23-cm) ovenproof pie dish.

7. Put 1 round in the base of the dish and add the chicken filling. Place the second round on top and press the edges together to seal.

8. Beat the remaining egg yolk and brush on top to glaze. Bake in the oven for about 40 minutes until golden brown.

Grilled Chicken Pieces with Dip

Ingredients

16 chicken wings

For the marinade:

Few dashes Tabasco sauce

4 tbsp oil

1 tbsp honey

1 tbsp ketchup

2 tbsp chili sauce

1 tbsp vinegar

Salt & freshly milled pepper

1 scallion (spring onion), finely chopped

For the mango dip:

1 mango

1 tbsp honey

1 tbsp rosemary leaves

Lime juice, to taste

Method

Prep and cook time: 45 min plus marinating time 12 hours

1. For the marinade, mix the Tabasco sauce, oil, honey, ketchup, chili sauce and vinegar. Season well with salt and pepper and stir in the scallions (spring onions).

2. Wash and dry the chicken pieces and brush with the marinade. Cover and marinate, preferably overnight. Then cook on a grill over a medium heat for 15–20 minutes, turning frequently.

3. For the mango dip, finely purée the flesh of a mango with 1 tablespoon honey and 1 tablespoon rosemary leaves. Add a little lime juice to taste.

4. Serve the chicken wings with a separate dish of mango dip.

Chicken Nuggets

Ingredients

1 lb 6 oz / 600 g chicken breast

Salt & freshly milled pepper

3–4 tbsp all-purpose (plain) flour

2 eggs

2 cups breadcrumbs, to coat

Fat for frying

Chili sauce or tomato ketchup

Method

Prep and cook time: 30 min

1. Wash the chicken breasts and pat dry. Cut into bite-size pieces and season with salt and pepper.

2. Lightly coat the chicken pieces with flour. Whisk the eggs in a bowl. Place the breadcrumbs on a plate. Coat the chicken pieces with egg, then roll in the breadcrumbs and press down well.

3. Fry the nuggets in hot fat for 3–4 minutes until the chicken is cooked. Drain on a paper towel. Serve with chili sauce or tomato ketchup.

Caribbean Chicken

Ingredients

4 boneless chicken breasts, skinned

1 onion, finely chopped

1 garlic clove, finely chopped

1 red bell pepper, de-seeded and finely chopped

1 green bell pepper, de-seeded and finely chopped

2 tbsp sunflower oil

¾ cup / 60 g grated coconut

Grated zest and juice of 1 lime

½ tsp paprika

½ tsp red chili paste

1 tsp salt

1 tbsp / 15 g butter

1 tsp apricot jam

Method

Prep and cook time: 1 hour

1. Preheat the oven to 375°F (190°C / Gas Mark 5). Put the chicken breasts between 2 sheets of plastic wrap (clingfilm) and, using a mallet or wooden rolling pin, beat the meat until flattened.

2. Heat the oil in a skillet (frying pan). Add the onion and garlic and fry over a medium heat for 2–3 minutes. Add the peppers and fry until softened. Stir in the coconut and remove the pan from the heat. Stir in the lime zest.

3. Place an equal amount of the vegetables in the center of each chicken breast. Fold the ends over the top of the filling and secure with toothpicks (cocktail sticks).

4. Put the paprika, chili paste and salt in a small bowl and mix together. Brush each chicken roll with the marinade.

5. Melt the butter in a roasting pan, add the chicken rolls and bake in the oven for 25–30 minutes until golden brown, basting from time to time.

6. Remove the chicken from the pan and keep warm. Stir the apricot jam and lime juice into the pan juices. Bring to a boil, reduce the heat, and simmer for 2–3 minutes, stirring all the time. Serve the chicken with the sauce poured over the top.

Chicken Cacciatore

Ingredients

1 onion, finely chopped

1 garlic clove, crushed

1 lb 8 oz / 650 g boneless chicken thighs, skinned

1 tbsp olive oil

1 tsp chopped fresh oregano, plus extra to garnish

½ tsp celery salt

Salt and pepper

7 tbsp white wine

14 oz / 400 g can chopped tomatoes

½ tsp sugar

Black olives, to garnish

Method

Prep and cook time: 40 mins

1. Cut the chicken into chunks. Heat the oil in a skillet (frying pan), add the onions, garlic and oregano and fry for about 3 minutes, until softened.

2. Add the chicken pieces, sprinkle in the celery salt and season with pepper. Cook for 10 minutes, turning occasionally, until lightly browned.

3. Pour in the wine and bring to a simmer. Add the tomatoes and sugar, cover with a lid and leave to simmer for 20 minutes until the chicken is tender and cooked through.

4. Serve the chicken garnished with black olives and oregano and accompany with pasta.

Coq au Vin

Ingredients

2 oz / ½ stick / 50 g butter

3 lb / 1.5 kg chicken, jointed into 6 or 8 pieces

5 oz / 150 g bacon, diced

2 garlic cloves, finely chopped

16 small onions

1 tbsp all purpose (plain) flour

1 bottle robust red wine

Salt and pepper

7 oz / 200 g button mushrooms, halved

Chicken broth (stock)

1 bouquet garni

Method

Prep and cook time: 50 min

1. Melt the butter in a large skillet (frying pan) and fry the chicken and bacon until lightly browned. Remove from the pan and set aside.

2. Add the garlic and onion to the pan and cook for about 5 minutes until softened. Stir in the flour.

3. Put the mushrooms into the pan with the onion and garlic and then add the bacon and chicken. Pour in the wine and enough chicken broth (stock) to cover the chicken. Add the bouquet garni.

4. Bring to a boil and simmer for about 30–40 minutes until the chicken is tender. For a thicker sauce, remove the chicken once it is cooked and keep warm. Cook the sauce over a high heat for a few minutes until the volume of liquid has reduced. Return the chicken back to the pan. Discard the bouquet garni before serving.

Chicken on Stir-fried Vegetables

Ingredients

1–2 tsp Chinese five-spice powder

2 limes

12–14 tbsp dark soy sauce

4 chicken breast fillets

11 oz / 300 g snow peas (mangetout), trimmed

1 medium sized zucchini (courgette), sliced

7 oz / 200 g carrots, peeled and cut into matchsticks

2 tbsp oil

½ tsp chili powder

Salt

Scant ½ cup / 100 ml vegetable broth (stock)

3–4 oz / 75–100 g pea sprouts (or bean sprouts if unavailable)

2 tbsp sesame seeds (toasted)

Method

Prep and cook time: 40 min

1. Wash the limes, remove the zest with a zester and chop finely and squeeze the limes. Mix the five-spice powder, the zest and juice of the limes, and 6–8 tbsps. of the soy sauce to make a marinade; marinate the chicken for about 15 minutes.

2. Broil (grill) the chicken under a medium heat until cooked through, for 3–5 minutes on each side (depending on thickness).

3. Meanwhile, heat the oil in a wok. Add the snow peas (mangetout) and stir-fry for 1 minute. Add the zucchini (courgette) and carrots and cook for a further 2 minutes. Add the chili powder, 2 tbsp soy sauce, and salt. Then add the broth (stock) and cook for a further 5 minutes.

4. Wash and drain the pea sprouts and add to the vegetables with the sesame seeds. Stir-fry for a further 2 minutes.

5. Slice the chicken and drizzle with the remaining soy sauce (or to taste). Serve the stir-fried vegetables onto plates and put the chicken on top.

Tandoori Chicken Kebabs

Ingredients

4 boneless chicken breasts, skinned

Salt and pepper

Juice of 1 lemon

2 garlic cloves

1 walnut-sized piece fresh ginger

1 cup / 200 g plain yogurt

2 tbsp vegetable oil

¼ tsp ground cumin

¼ tsp ground nutmeg

¼ tsp ground coriander

¼ tsp black pepper

¼ tsp paprika

For the raita:

1 cucumber

1¼ cups / 250 g plain yogurt

1 tbsp finely chopped fresh parsley

1 tbsp finely chopped fresh mint

½ tsp ground caraway

½ tsp ground coriander

Salt and pepper

Mint leaves, to garnish

Method

Prep and cook time: 40 min plus 12 hours marinating

1. Cut the chicken into bite-sized pieces and put in a shallow dish. Season with salt and pepper and drizzle over the lemon juice.

2. To make the marinade, crush the garlic. Peel and grate the ginger. Put in a bowl, add the yogurt, oil and the spices and mix together.

3. Generously brush the chicken with the marinade and cover the dish with foil. Leave to marinate in the refrigerator overnight.

4. To make the raita, peel, remove the seeds and grate the cucumber. Put in a bowl, add the yogurt, parsley, mint, caraway and coriander, and season to taste with salt and pepper. Leave to stand for 1 hour.

5. Preheat the broiler (grill) and cover the rack with foil. Skewer the chicken pieces on to kebab sticks, reserving the marinade.

6. Cook the kebabs for about 8–10 minutes (or until cooked through), turning halfway through the cooking time and brushing with the reserved marinade.

7. Serve the Tandoori Chicken Kebabs with the Raita, garnished with mint leaves.

Chicken with Bacon and Potato-Watercress Salad

Ingredients

For the potato salad:

1¾ lb / 800 g new potatoes, peeled and halved if large

2 tbsp walnut oil

4 tbsp vegetable oil

3 tbsp cider vinegar

1 tsp dry mustard

Salt and freshly ground pepper, to taste

½ bunch scallions (spring onions), thinly sliced

For the chicken:

4 skinless boneless chicken breasts, halved lengthwise

Salt and freshly ground pepper, to taste

1 tbsp olive oil

1 tsp butter

4 slices bacon

1 tbsp finely chopped fresh parsley

1 bunch watercress, trimmed

3–4 lettuce leaves, torn into bite-size pieces

Method

Prep and cook time: 50 min

1. Cook the potatoes in boiling salted water until tender, about 25 minutes. Drain and cut into bite-size pieces.

2. Whisk the oils, vinegar, mustard, salt and pepper in a large bowl. Add the potatoes and scallions (spring onions), mix well and let stand to absorb the flavors.

3. Meanwhile, heat the broiler (grill) and season the chicken with salt and pepper. Put under the broiler and cook thoroughly. Heat the oil and butter in a skillet and fry the bacon until crisp. Take out and drain on paper towels, leaving the fat in the skillet.

4. Arrange the potato salad on plates with the watercress and lettuce, add the chicken and bacon and serve.

Prosciutto-wrapped Chicken Breasts

Ingredients

4 skinless boneless chicken breasts

Salt and freshly ground pepper, to taste

8 sage leaves, plus additional leaves to garnish

4 large paper-thin slices prosciutto

12 oz / 350 g snow peas (mangetout)

Heaping 1 cup / 150 g frozen peas

1 scallion (spring onion), chopped

1 tbsp olive oil

½ cup / 125 ml meat, poultry or vegetable broth (stock)

¼ cup / 50 ml light cream

2 tbsp lemon juice

Method

Prep and cook time: 30 min

1. Season the chicken breasts with salt and pepper and place 2 sage leaves on each one. Wrap a slice of prosciutto around each breast and secure with toothpicks.

2. Bring a saucepan of salted water to a boil; add the snow peas (mangetout) and green peas and cook until bright green, about 5 minutes. Place in a colander under cold running water to stop the cooking; set aside.

3. Heat the oil in a skillet over medium heat; add the chicken and cook until browned on both sides and no longer pink in the center, about 10 minutes. Transfer to a plate and keep warm.

4. Return the skillet to the heat and stir in the broth (stock) and cream. Add the peas, snow peas and scallions (spring onions) and heat through. Add the lemon juice and season with salt and pepper. To serve, thickly slice the chicken breasts and serve with the peas and cream sauce. Garnish with sage leaves.

Chicken with Lime Butter

Ingredients

12 oz / 350 g carrots, sliced

7 oz / 200 g snow peas (mangetout), trimmed

2 cloves garlic

2 tbsp lime juice

1 tsp lime zest

3 oz / 1½ stick / 90 g soft butter

4 chicken breast fillets (skinned)

Salt & freshly milled pepper

Some basil leaves, shredded

Lime slices, to garnish

Method

Prep and cook time: 30 min

1. Blanch the carrots in boiling, salted water for 3–4 minutes, then drain, refresh in cold water, and drain thoroughly.

2. Peel the garlic. Mix the lime juice and zest with 2 oz / 50 g of the butter. Crush the garlic into the butter and season with a little salt. Mix well.

3. Season the chicken with salt and pepper. Put into a baking dish and spread with the garlic and lime butter. Cook under a preheated broiler (grill) for 5–10 minutes each side.

4. To serve, heat the vegetables in the rest of the butter and season with salt and pepper. Scatter the vegetables with basil and put on plates with the chicken breasts. Serve at once, garnished with lime slices.

Tomato Stuffed Chicken Breasts

Ingredients

4 oz / 115 g dried tomatoes in oil

4 tbsp chopped fresh basil

3 tbsp grated Parmesan cheese

1 tbsp toasted pine nuts

3 tbsp olive oil

Salt and pepper

2 large red bell peppers

1 tbsp sunflower oil, for greasing

4 boneless chicken breasts, skinned

1 tbsp lemon juice

8 slices bacon

Method

Prep and cook time: 45 min

1. Preheat the oven to 375°F (190°C / Gas Mark 5). Drain the tomatoes and finely chop.

2. To make the pesto, put the basil, Parmesan cheese, pine nuts and olive oil in a food processor and blend together to form a purée. Season with salt and pepper.

3. Remove the stems, core and seeds from the peppers and cut into quarters. Place, skin side up, in a lightly greased ovenproof dish. Brush a little oil on the peppers.

4. Make a horizontal cut along each chicken breast to form a pocket. Rub each breast, inside and out, with the lemon juice, salt and pepper. Fill the pockets with the tomatoes and pesto.

5. Wrap each chicken breast with two strips of bacon and put in the prepared dish with the peppers.

6. Bake in the oven for about 25 minutes, until tender.

Chicken Meatballs

Ingredients

3 slices day-old white bread

¾ cup / 200 ml whipping cream

1 tbsp chopped scallions (spring onions),
plus extra to garnish

1 lb 7 oz / 650 g ground (minced)
chicken

3 tbsp lemon juice

2 tbsp chopped fresh lemon balm or
lemon thyme

2 tbsp chopped fresh mint

Salt and pepper

6 tbsp fresh breadcrumbs

2 tbsp sesame seeds

4 tbsp vegetable oil

Carrot ribbons, to garnish

Method

Prep and cook time: 30 min

1. Tear the bread into small pieces and put in a large bowl. Add the cream and leave until softened.

2. Finely chop the scallions (spring onions). Add to the bread with the chicken, lemon juice, lemon balm or thyme and the mint and mix together. Season with salt and pepper.

3. With damp hands, form the meat mixture into meatballs. You should make about 20.

4. Put the breadcrumbs and sesame seeds in a shallow dish and mix together. Coat the meatballs in the mixture.

5. Heat the oil in a skillet (frying pan), add the meatballs and fry for about 5 minutes, browning all sides, until the chicken is thoroughly cooked. Serve garnished with the scallions and carrot ribbons.

Chicken Saltimbocca

Ingredients

3 tbsp olive oil, plus extra to grease

4 boneless chicken breasts, skinned

7 oz / 200 g mozzarella cheese

8 slices prosciutto

8 sage leaves

Salt and pepper

7 tbsp dry white wine

Small bunch watercress, to garnish

Method

Prep and cook time: 35 min

1. Preheat the oven to 400°F (200°C / Gas Mark 6). Lightly oil a roasting pan.

2. Slice each chicken breast in half horizontally. Put them in plastic wrap (clingfilm) and beat with a meat mallet or wooden rolling pin to flatten slightly.

3. Heat 2 tbsp oil in a large skillet (frying pan) and briefly brown the chicken pieces on both sides. Remove from the pan and place in the prepared roasting pan.

4. Slice the mozzarella cheese. Put a prosciutto slice, a sage leaf and 2 slices of mozzarella cheese on each chicken breast. Season lightly with salt and pepper.

5. Cook in the oven for about 8 minutes until golden brown and cooked through.

6. Remove the chicken pieces from the roasting pan. Add the wine to the pan and cook on the hob, stirring all the time to deglaze the pan, until the sauce has reduced slightly.

7. Serve the Saltimbocca with the sauce poured over the top and garnish with the watercress.

Chicken with Lemon and Capers
on a Bed of Vegetables

Ingredients

1 lb / 450 g asparagus

1 lb / 450 g string (runner) beans

Salt and pepper

12 oz / 350 g snow peas (mangetout)

4 boneless chicken breasts, skinned

6 tbsp / 75 g butter

4 tbsp lemon juice

4 tbsp small capers

Grated lemon zest, to garnish

Method

Prep and cook time: 30 min

1. Peel the bottom third from the asparagus stalks and trim the ends. Top and tail the beans.

2. Put the asparagus and beans in a saucepan of boiling salted water and boil for about 6 minutes.

3. Add the snow peas (mangetout) to the pan and continue boiling for a further 4 minutes. Drain well, immerse the vegetables in cold water and drain again. Return to the pan.

4. Season the chicken breasts with salt and pepper. Heat 2 tbsp (25 g) butter in a skillet (frying pan) until melted. Add the chicken breasts and fry for about 5 minutes on each side until cooked.

5. Add the remaining 4 tbsp (2 oz / 50 g) butter to the vegetables and heat until melted and the vegetables are hot. Add the lemon juice and season with the salt and pepper.

6. To serve, divide the vegetables and butter sauce between 4 serving plates. Put a chicken breast on top of each and sprinkle with the capers and lemon zest to garnish.

Chow Mein
(Egg Noodles with Chicken and Vegetables)

Ingredients

8 oz / 225 g dried egg noodles

4 tsp sesame oil

4 oz / 100 g chicken breast, cut into fine strips

3 tbsp vegetable oil

1 tbsp finely chopped garlic

½ cup / 50 g snow peas (mangetout), finely sliced

⅓ cup / 50 g cooked ham, finely shredded

4 tsp light soy sauce

1 tbsp rice wine

Salt and freshly milled pepper

½ tsp sugar

3 tbsp chopped scallions (spring onions)

For the marinade:

2 tsp light soy sauce

2 tsp rice wine, or dry sherry

1 tsp sesame oil

Salt & freshly milled white pepper

Method
Prep and cook time: 40 min

1. Cook the noodles in a large pan of boiling water for 3–5 minutes, then drain and refresh in cold water. Drain thoroughly, toss with 3 teaspoons of the sesame oil and set aside.

2. Combine the chicken with all the marinade ingredients, mix well and marinate for about 10 minutes.

3. Heat a skillet or wok over a high heat. Add 1 tablespoon of the vegetable oil and when very hot and slightly smoking add the shredded chicken. Stir-fry for about 2 minutes and then transfer to a plate.

4. Reheat the wok until it is very hot, then add the remaining vegetable oil. When the oil is slightly smoking add the garlic and stir-fry for 10 seconds. Then add the snow peas (mangetout) and ham and stir-fry for about 1 minute.

5. Add the chicken and any juices, stir-fry for 3–4 minutes until the chicken is nearly cooked then add the rice wine or sherry, salt, pepper, sugar and scallions. Stir-fry for 2 minutes.

6. Add the noodles and remaining sesame oil and give the mixture a few final stirs to reheat the noodles. Turn onto a warm platter and serve at once.

Chicken Tikka Masala

Ingredients

1 oven-ready chicken, 3 lb / 1.4 kg, cut into 6-8 pieces

1 lemon

Salt & freshly milled pepper

For the marinade:

2 tsp freshly grated ginger

2 cloves garlic, crushed

2 cups / 500 g yogurt

2 tbsp vegetable oil

2 tbsp paprika

Spice mixture: ½ tsp ground cumin, black pepper, chili powder and curcuma (turmeric)

1 tbsp cilantro (coriander) leaves, chopped

Method
Prep and cook time: 1 hour 15 min plus 8 hours to marinate

1. Score the surface of the chicken pieces to a depth of ¼ inch (0.5 cm) and put into a shallow dish. Sprinkle with pepper, salt and the juice of a lemon. Let stand for about 30 minutes.

2. Mix all the spices for the marinade with the yogurt. Coat the chicken pieces generously with the marinade and seal the dish with aluminum foil. Leave in the refrigerator for 8 hours or overnight.

3. Preheat the oven to 350°F (180°C / Gas Mark 4). Line a cookie sheet with aluminum foil and put the chicken pieces on the sheet. Cook in the oven for 35–40 minutes, brushing frequently with marinade (using about a quarter), and adding a little water if necessary.

4. Heat the remaining marinade in a large pan and add the chicken pieces. Continue to heat very gently for 5 minutes, then sprinkle with cilantro (coriander) and serve with rice.

Spicy Chicken with Almonds

Ingredients

8 boneless chicken thighs, skinned

Salt and pepper

5 garlic cloves

2 tsp medium curry powder

2 tsp paprika

½ tsp ground cinnamon

4 tbsp vegetable oil

2 cups / 375 g couscous

2 cups / 450 ml hot vegetable broth (stock)

2 oz / ½ stick / 50 g butter

4 tbsp toasted flaked almonds, to garnish

Method

Prep and cook time: 1 hour 15 min

1. Cut each chicken thigh into 3 pieces. Put into a large bowl and season generously with salt and pepper.

2. Crush the garlic and put in a small bowl. Add the curry powder, paprika, cinnamon and 3 tbsp oil and mix together.

3. Spoon the mixture over the chicken and turn to coat all over. Cover and leave to marinate for 30 minutes.

4. Preheat the oven to 400°F (200°C / Gas Mark 6) Heat the remaining oil in a flameproof casserole dish. Add the chicken and cook over a medium heat for 10 minutes until browned all over.

5. Cover the dish and cook in the oven for 20 minutes until the chicken is cooked.

6. Put the couscous into an ovenproof dish. Just before the chicken is cooked, pour in the hot stock and add 1 tsp salt. Stir and leave for 10 minutes until the stock has been absorbed.

7. Fluff up the couscous with a fork. Dice the butter and dot over the couscous. Serve the spiced chicken, garnished with toasted flaked almonds, and accompany with the couscous.

Chicken with Ricotta Stuffing

Ingredients

1 lb 12 oz / 800 g small, new potatoes

Salt and pepper

4 garlic cloves

5 oz / 150 g ricotta cheese

4 boneless chicken thighs, with skin on

½ cup / 125 ml olive oil

1 lb / 450 g string (runner) beans

3 scallions (spring onions)

2 oz / 4 tbsp / 50 g butter

4 tbsp chopped fresh parsley

Method

Prep and cook time: 1 hour

1. Preheat the oven to 375°F (190°C / Gas Mark 5). Cook the potatoes in a saucepan of boiling salted water for 20–25 minutes until tender. Drain well.

2. Finely chop the garlic and put in a bowl. Add 2 tbsp oil and the ricotta cheese. Season with salt and pepper and mix together.

3. Loosen the skin on the chicken thighs by running your fingers between the skin and the meat. Spoon the ricotta mixture under the skin, dividing it equally among the thighs. Season with salt and pepper.

4. Heat 2 tbsp of the oil in a roasting pan. Add the chicken thighs and sear on all sides. Roast in the oven for about 30 minutes, basting from time to time.

5. Cut the potatoes into wedges and place in a lightly greased casserole dish. Brush with the remaining oil and sprinkle with pepper. Bake in the oven for 10 minutes until you can pierce the potatoes easily with a fork.

6. Meanwhile, cook the beans in salted boiling water for about 10 minutes until tender. Drain well.

7. Finely chop the scallions (spring onions). Melt the butter in a saucepan, add the scallions and fry for 4–5 minutes. Stir in the chopped parsley. Season with salt and pepper.

8. Arrange the potatoes, beans and chicken thighs on the serving plates and serve with the scallions spooned over the top.

Chicken in Basil Sauce

Ingredients

1 lb / 450 g green ribbon noodles

4 oz / 120 g shallots

1 lb 8 oz / 675g boneless chicken breasts, skinned

1 lb 12 oz / 800 g tomatoes

1 cup / 25 g basil leaves

3 tbsp vegetable oil

Generous ¾ cup / 200 g crème fraîche

7 tbsp whipping cream

Salt and pepper

2 oz / 50 g Parmesan cheese, half grated, half sliced

Method

Prep and cook time: 30 min

1. Cook the noodles according to the package directions until tender but still with a slight bite. Drain well.

2. Meanwhile, finely chop the shallots. Cut the chicken into cubes.

3. Blanch the tomatoes in boiling water, immerse in cold water and remove the skins. Coarsely chop the flesh.

4. Reserve a few of the basil leaves. Chop the rest into thin strips.

5. Heat the oil in a wok and fry the shallots until softened. Add the chicken and stir for about 1 minute.

6. Stir in the tomatoes, crème fraîche and cream. Add the basil and season with salt and pepper. Continue to fry over a high heat for 4 minutes (or until the chicken is thoroughly cooked), stirring continuously.

7. Add the drained noodles and mix together. Garnish with slices of Parmesan cheese and the reserved basil leaves and serve the grated cheese separately for sprinkling on top.

Persian Chicken

Ingredients

1 cup / 200 g yellow split lentils

4 cups / 1 liter water

1 tsp salt

4 boneless chicken breasts, skinned

1 large onion

2 garlic cloves

2 tbsp / 25 g butter

2 tsp garam masala

1 tsp turmeric

1 tsp hot chili powder

7 oz / 200 g canned chopped tomatoes

Fresh spinach leaves, to garnish

Method

Prep and cook time: 1 hour 15 min

1. Put the lentils in a saucepan with the water and salt. Bring to the boil, then cover and simmer for 30 minutes until the lentils are tender and have absorbed most of the water.

2. Meanwhile, cut the chicken breasts into bite-sized pieces. Chop the onion and crush the garlic.

3. Melt the butter in a large skillet (frying pan) or flameproof casserole. Add the chicken and fry for 5 minutes until golden on all sides.

4. Add the onion, garlic, garam masala, turmeric and chili powder and gently fry for 5 minutes until the onion is softened.

5. Add the tomatoes, cooked lentils and 4 tbsp water. Cover and simmer gently for 30 minutes until the chicken is tender. Serve with noodles or rice, if wished, and garnish with fresh spinach leaves.

Chicken Jalfrezi

Ingredients

1 lb 2 oz / 500 g chicken breast fillets

1 tbsp Worcestershire sauce

3 onions

7 oz / 200 g sugarsnap peas

1 cup / 150 g frozen peas

2 red chilis, or more according to taste

3 tbsp oil

A good pinch of brown mustard seeds

A good pinch of cumin seeds

A good pinch of ground cumin

A pinch of ground coriander

A good pinch of ground turmeric

$\frac{2}{3}$–$\frac{3}{4}$ cup / 150–200 ml coconut cream, to taste

Salt & freshly milled pepper

Mint leaves

Method

Prep and cook time: 25 min

1. Cut the meat into thin strips and mix with the Worcestershire sauce. Peel, halve and slice the onions. Wash and trim the sugarsnap peas. Thaw the frozen peas. Slit the chilis open lengthways, remove the seeds and inner ribs, and finely chop the flesh.

2. Heat the oil in a skillet and fry the mustard seeds and cumin seeds, stirring, for about 30 seconds, until they start to pop. Add the onions and chilis and fry, stirring, until the onions are lightly browned.

3. Stir in the meat, ground spices, Worcestershire sauce, sugarsnap peas and thawed frozen peas and season with salt and pepper. Add 1 cup of water, bring to a boil and cook over a medium heat for a further 3–5 minutes, stirring, until the meat and vegetables are just cooked.

4. Add coconut cream to taste. Sprinkle with mint and serve with rice.

Chicken
with Oyster Sauce and Noodles

Ingredients

1 lb / 400 g udon noodles

1½ lb / 600 g skinless boneless chicken breasts, chopped into bite-size pieces

Salt and freshly ground pepper, to taste

5 tbsp sesame oil, divided

4-inch / 10-cm piece lemongrass

1 clove garlic, minced

1 scallion (spring onion), finely chopped

3 tbsp / 40 ml oyster sauce

2 tbsp light soy sauce

1 tsp sugar

Method

Prep and cook time: 40 min plus 30 min marinading time

1. Cook the noodles in boiling salted water according to package instructions; drain and set aside.

2. In a small bowl, mix the chicken with salt, pepper, lemongrass and 2 tbsp of the sesame oil; marinate for 30 minutes.

3. Heat the remaining 3 tbsp oil in a wok or large skillet and stir-fry the garlic and the spring onions for 30 seconds. Add the chicken and fry all together until the chicken is cooked. Season with oyster sauce, soy sauce and sugar; discard the lemongrass stalk.

4. Toss the noodles with the chicken and the sauce and heat through; serve at once.

Chicken and Asparagus Risotto

Ingredients

1 lb / 450 g asparagus

1 garlic clove

5 tbsp olive oil

4 boneless chicken breasts, skinned

Salt and pepper

¾ cup / 150 g risotto rice

2 cups / 475 ml vegetable broth (stock)

1 tbsp / 15 g butter

½ cup / 50 g freshly grated Parmesan cheese

1 tbsp fresh thyme leaves

Method
Prep and cook time: 45 min

1. Peel the bottom third from the asparagus stalks and cut the spears into bite-sized pieces. Crush the garlic.

2. Heat 2 tbsp oil in a large skillet (frying pan), add the garlic and fry for 30 seconds. Add the asparagus, fry for 1-2 minutes, then add a little water and cook very gently until tender but still with a slight bite. Remove from the skillet and set aside.

3. Cut the chicken breasts into dice. Heat 2 tbsp oil in the skillet, add the chicken pieces and fry until browned on all sides and cooked through. Season with salt and pepper and remove from the pan.

4. Heat the remaining 1 tbsp oil in the pan. Add the rice and stir until slightly translucent, then add a ladleful of stock and stir until it has been absorbed. Continue in this way, gradually adding more stock and stirring all the time, until the rice is tender but still has a slight bite and the risotto is creamy. This will take about 20 minutes.

5. Stir in the chicken and asparagus and add the butter and grated Parmesan cheese. Season to taste with salt and pepper, stir in the thyme leaves and serve.

Jambalaya

Ingredients

4 boneless chicken breasts, skinned

1 onion

1 celery stalk

2 garlic cloves

3 scallions (spring onions)

2 red bell peppers

2 red chilies

3 tbsp olive oil

9 oz / 1¼ cup / 250 g long grain rice

2 cups / 475 ml chicken broth (stock)

1 bay leaf

Salt and pepper

6 oz / 150 g canned chopped tomatoes

2 tbsp chopped fresh cilantro (coriander)

Method
Prep and cook time: 50 min

1. Cut the chicken into slices. Chop the onion, celery and garlic. Slice the scallions (spring onions) into rings. Finely slice the red peppers and chilies, discarding the core and seeds.

2. Heat the oil in a large skillet (frying pan), add the onion, garlic and scallions and fry for 2–3 minutes. Add the chicken and continue to fry for 1–2 minutes.

3. Stir in the celery, red pepper, chilies and rice. Pour in the chicken stock and add the bay leaf. Season with salt and pepper.

4. Cover the pan and simmer for about 20 minutes, stirring occasionally. When the rice is cooked, add the tomatoes and cilantro (coriander) leaves. Before serving, season to taste with cumin, salt and pepper.

Rigatoni with Chicken and Broccoli

Ingredients

1 lb / 400 g rigatoni

14 oz / 400 g grilled chicken

14oz / 400 g broccoli florets

1½ oz / 40 g sun-dried tomatoes

2 cloves garlic

4 tsp oil

1 lemon

2 tbsp black olives, chopped

Salt & freshly milled pepper

2–3 tbsp chopped parsley

Method

Prep and cook time: 30 min

1. Cook the pasta in plenty of boiling, salted water until al dente.

2. Meanwhile remove the chicken meat from the bones and cut into pieces.

3. Blanch the broccoli in boiling, salted water for 3–4 minutes, then refresh in cold water and drain.

4. Chop the sun-dried tomatoes. Peel and crush the garlic. Heat the oil in a skillet and add the garlic, tomatoes and chicken. Season lightly with salt and pepper. Grate a little lemon peel into the pan, squeeze in the lemon juice and warm over a low heat for 8–10 minutes.

5. Add the broccoli and heat very gently for a further 5 minutes or so. Mix in the chopped olives and parsley and reheat.

6. Season to taste with salt and pepper. Then mix with the drained pasta and serve hot.

Penne with Chicken and Peas

Ingredients

1 shallot

1 garlic clove

2 chicken breasts

2 tbsp / 30 g butter

1 tbsp flour

$^2/_3$ cup / 150 ml chicken broth (stock)

$^1/_3$ cup / 80 ml whipping cream

1 cup / 150 g frozen peas, defrosted

1 lemon

1 lb / 450 g penne

1 tbsp finely chopped parsley

Salt and freshly ground pepper

Method

Prep and cook time: 30 min

1. Peel and finely chop the shallot and garlic.

2. Wash the chicken breasts and pat dry. Slice into thin strips.

3. Sauté the chicken, shallot and garlic in hot butter. Sprinkle the flour on top. Mix and sauté briefly.

4. Add the broth (stock) and cream while stirring. Season with salt and pepper and bring to a boil. Add the peas and simmer over low heat for about 10 minutes. Stir occasionally.

5. Zest the lemon and squeeze out the juice.

6. Cook the penne in well-salted boiling water until al dente.

7. Add the parsley and lemon zest to the cream sauce. Season with a little lemon juice, salt and pepper.

8. Divide the well-drained pasta among the plates. Pour the sauce over the top and serve.

Chicken and Mushroom Tagliatelle

Ingredients

1 small onion

2 carrots

3 boneless chicken breasts, skinned

2 sprigs fresh thyme

1 cup / 225 ml water

2 tbsp dry sherry (optional)

Salt and pepper

1 lb / 450 g tagliatelle

9 oz / 250 ml button mushrooms

2 garlic cloves

2 oz / ½ stick / 50 g butter

1 tbsp all-purpose (plain) white flour

Chopped fresh flat leaf parsley, to garnish

Method

Prep and cook time: 30 min

1. Cut the onion into quarters and the carrots into batons. Put in a large saucepan with the chicken, thyme, water and sherry, if using. Season generously with salt and pepper.

2. Bring to the boil, then reduce the heat and simmer for 15 minutes until the chicken is tender when pierced with a fork. Add more water during cooking if necessary. Drain, set the chicken and vegetables aside and reserve the stock.

3. Put the tagliatelle into a saucepan of boiling salted water and cook according to the packet instructions until tender but still with a slight bite.

4. Meanwhile, slice the mushrooms and crush the garlic. Melt the butter in a skillet (frying pan), add the mushrooms and garlic and fry for 5 minutes until softened.

5. Add the flour and cook for 1 minute. Gradually add the stock, stirring all the time, and cook until the sauce has thickened. Add the chicken and vegetables and heat through.

6. Drain the tagliatelle and divide between 4 serving plates. Put the chicken and mushroom mixture on top and serve sprinkled with parsley, to garnish.

Chicken Breasts in Coconut Milk

Ingredients

1 carrot

1 leek

2 celery stalks

1 bay leaf

1 red chili

2 boneless chicken breasts, with skin on

1 tbsp / 15 g butter

1 tbsp sugar

2 tsp finely chopped fresh ginger

1 cup / 225 ml coconut milk

Salt and pepper

6 oz / 150 g corn salad (lamb's lettuce)

2 tbsp balsamic vinegar

3 tbsp olive oil

1 cup / 35 g basil leaves

Method

Prep and cook time: 45 min

1. Roughly chop the carrot, leek and celery stalk and put in a wide saucepan. Add the bay leaf. Finely chop the chili, discarding the seeds, and set aside.

2. Lay the chicken breasts on top of the vegetables, add enough water just to cover the meat and bring to a gentle boil. Simmer for about 15 minutes and remove from the heat.

3. Melt the butter and sugar in a clean pan over high heat and allow to caramelize slightly. As soon as the sugar starts to caramelize add the chopped chili and ginger. Pour in the coconut milk and cook until reduced slightly. Season with salt and pepper.

5. Arrange the corn salad (lamb's lettuce) on a serving dish. Dress with the olive oil and balsamic vinegar.

6. Coarsely chop the basil leaves and add to the coconut milk sauce.

7. Remove the chicken breasts from the pan and slice. Add to the serving plates and drizzle over the sauce to serve.

Chicken with Lime and Mint

Ingredients

6 tbsp lime juice

1 tbsp fish sauce

2 tsp sugar

4 boneless chicken breasts, skinned

1 red chili

12 oz / 350 g rice noodles

Salt

1 carrot

1 small zucchini (courgette)

1 cup / 20 g fresh mint leaves

3 tbsp olive oil

Lime zest, to garnish

Method

Prep and cook time: 1 hour

1. Put 3 tbsp of the lime juice, the fish sauce and sugar in a bowl and mix together. Rub into the chicken breasts. Leave to marinate for about 30 minutes, turning from time to time. Meanwhile, finely chop the chili, discarding the seeds, and set aside.

2. Put the noodles into a saucepan of boiling salted water and cook according to the packet instructions until tender but still with a slight bite. Drain well, rinse under cold water and drain well again.

3. Cut the carrot and zucchini (courgette) lengthways and cut into thin ribbons. Use a mandolin vegetable slicer if available.

4. Put the noodles, carrot ribbons, zucchini ribbons and mint leaves in a large bowl. Mix 1 tbsp oil with the remaining lime juice. Add to the bowl and toss together. Put into serving bowls.

5. Heat the remaining oil in a skillet (frying pan). Remove the chicken from the marinade, add to the pan and fry for about 5 minutes on each side or until cooked through.

6. Thickly slice the chicken breasts width ways and arrange on top of the noodles. Sprinkle with the chopped chili and serve garnished with lime zest.

Spinach Chicken Salad

Ingredients

2 boneless chicken breasts, skinned

2 tbsp light soy sauce

2 nori seaweed leaves

4 oz / 115 g cooked ham

1 red bell pepper

1 lb / 450 g fresh, baby spinach

4 tbsp sesame oil

2 tbsp rice wine vinegar

Salt and pepper

2 tbsp sunflower oil

2 tbsp sesame seeds

Method

Prep and cook time: 40 min

1. Cut the chicken breasts into bite-sized pieces and put in a bowl. Add the soy sauce and leave to marinate for 20 minutes.

2. Meanwhile, slice the nori leaves and ham into thin strips. Core and finely slice the red pepper, discarding the core and seeds.

3. Rinse the spinach and shake to remove excess water.

4. To make the dressing, put the sesame oil, rice wine vinegar, salt and pepper in a jug and whisk together.

5. Heat the sunflower oil in a skillet (frying pan), add the chicken pieces and fry until golden brown all over and cooked through.

6. Mix the spinach with the red pepper and toss in the dressing. Add more seasoning if wished. Carefully toss the chicken with the spinach.

7. Arrange the salad on serving plates. Garnish with the ham and nori strips and sprinkle the sesame seeds on top. Serve at once.

Chicken and Mango Salad

Ingredients

1 cucumber

2 scallions (spring onions)

3½ oz / 100 g bean sprouts

Salt and pepper

1 mango

4 smoked (cooked) boneless chicken breasts

6 tbsp French dressing

3 tbsp sweet chili sauce

4 Little Gem lettuces

Method

Prep and cook time: 20 min

1. Cut the cucumber in half lengthways and then into slices. Shred the scallions (spring onions). Put the cucumber and scallions into a large bowl and add the bean sprouts. Season with salt and pepper.

2. Peel and slice the mango flesh either side of the stone, and then cut into thin slices.

3. Shred the chicken. Add the chicken and mango to the salad ingredients and mix together.

4. Pour the French dressing into a screw-topped jar, add the sweet chili sauce and shake together. Toss the dressing into the salad.

5. Arrange the lettuce leaves in the base of a large salad bowl. Spoon the salad on top and serve.

Chicken Caesar Salad

Ingredients

4 garlic cloves

2 egg yolks

2 anchovy fillets

2 tbsp lemon juice

Salt and pepper

8 tbsp olive oil

2 tbsp chopped fresh parsley

½ cup / 50 g grated Parmesan cheese

2 boneless chicken breasts, skinned

2 tbsp vegetable oil

3 slices day-old white bread

4 oz / 1 stick / 120 g butter

1 romaine (cos) lettuce

Method

Prep and cook time: 25 min

1. For the dressing, crush 3 garlic cloves and put in a bowl with the egg yolks.

2. Rinse the anchovies in cool water and chop finely. Add to the egg yolks with the lemon juice, salt and pepper. Beat until creamy.

3. Sir in the oil, drop by drop, until the dressing thickens.

4. Add the parsley and cheese and mix together. Set aside.

5. Season the chicken with salt and pepper. Heat the oil in a skillet (frying pan) and fry the chicken for about 5 minutes on each side or until cooked through. Remove the chicken from the skillet and set aside.

6. Cut the bread into small cubes. Wipe the skillet with paper towels and rub the remaining garlic clove over base. Add the butter and fry the bread cubes until crunchy. Remove the cubes from the pan.

7. Tear the lettuce leaves into bite-sized pieces and toss together with the dressing. Slice the chicken diagonally into slices and serve alongside the salad. Sprinkle the bread croûtons on top to garnish.

Penne
with White Beans and Pesto

Ingredients

1 lb / 450 g penne

1¼ cups / 250 g canned white beans

1 cup / 20 g fresh basil leaves

1 cup / 20 g arugula (rocket)

1 sprig parsley

1 garlic clove

½ cup / 50 g pine nuts

About 3 tbsp olive oil

1 lemon

¼ cup / 25 g hard cheese

Salt and freshly ground pepper

Method
Prep and cook time: 20 min

1. Boil the penne in salted water until al dente.

2. Put the beans in a sieve. Rinse and drain.

3. Rinse the basil, arugula (rocket) and parsley leaves and shake dry. Discard any discolored leaves. Put the leaves in a food processor.

4. Peel the garlic clove and add it to the herbs along with the pine nuts. Pour in the olive oil and 1–2 tbsp of the penne cooking water. Purée until smooth.

5. Remove the zest from the lemon. Squeeze out the juice. Season the pesto with the lemon juice, salt and pepper.

6. Put the beans in with the penne during the last 2 minutes of cooking time. Drain.

7. Combine the pesto with the beans and penne. Divide among the plates. Sprinkle with the lemon zest and hard cheese. Serve.

Spaghetti alla Puttanesca

Ingredients

1 cup / 100 g black olives, pitted

6 anchovy fillets

4 garlic cloves

2 dried chili peppers

3 tbsp olive oil

2 cups / 400 g canned tomatoes, chopped

1 tbsp capers

1 lb / 450 g spaghetti

Salt and freshly ground pepper

Method
Prep and cook time: 25 min

1. Coarsely chop the olives and the anchovies.

2. Peel and finely chop the garlic. Sauté in hot oil for about 2 minutes with the chili peppers and the anchovies.

3. Add the tomatoes and simmer gently for about 10 minutes.

4. Cook the spaghetti in well-salted boiling water until al dente.

5. Add the capers and olives to the sauce. Season with salt and pepper.

6. Combine the sauce with the well-drained spaghetti. Serve.

Spinach Cannelloni

Ingredients

Olive oil, for the baking dish

9 oz / 250 g cannelloni tubes (no pre-cook type)

For the filling:

6 cups / 500 g spinach

2 cups / 200 g ricotta cheese

1 egg

Nutmeg

Salt and freshly ground pepper

For the tomatoes:

½ lb / 225 g tomatoes

1 shallot

1 garlic clove

1 tbsp olive oil

For the béchamel sauce:

1 tbsp butter

1 tbsp flour

1 cup / 250 ml milk

¾ cup / 75 g freshly grated hard cheese

Salt and freshly ground pepper

Method

Prep and cook time: 1 hour

1. Lightly grease an ovenproof dish with a little olive oil. Preheat the oven to 400°F (200°C / Gas Mark 6).

2. Wash the spinach well, put into a pan dripping wet and heat over a medium heat until it wilts. Drain, refresh in cold water, drain again and squeeze out excess water.

3. Roughly chop the spinach and mix with the mashed ricotta. Stir in the egg and season with salt, pepper and nutmeg.

4. Spoon the mixture into the cannelloni tubes and place them side by side in the baking dish.

5. Drop the tomatoes into boiling water for a few seconds, refresh in cold water, then skin, quarter, deseed and chop roughly.

6. Peel and finely chop the shallot and garlic. Heat the oil and sauté the shallot and garlic then add the tomatoes and cook over a medium heat for about 5 minutes.

7. For the béchamel sauce, melt the butter, stir in the flour and cook for a couple of minutes without browning. Then gradually stir in the milk. Simmer for 10 minutes, season with salt and pepper and stir in half of the hard. cheese

8. Spread the tomatoes on the cannelloni. Pour the sauce over and sprinkle with the rest of the hard cheese. Dot with butter and bake for about 30 minutes.

Tomato and Mozzarella Lasagne

Ingredients

Olive oil, for the baking dish

2 garlic cloves, finely chopped

2 cups / 400 g canned tomatoes, chopped

2 sprigs basil

¾ lb / 350 g mozzarella cheese

12 lasagne sheets, no precook type

¾ cup / 75 g hard cheese

Salt and freshly ground pepper

For the béchamel sauce:

2 oz / 4 tbps /50 g butter

3 tbsp flour

2 cups / 500 ml milk

Salt and freshly ground pepper

Method

Prep and cook time: 1 hour 20 min

1. Lightly grease an ovenproof dish with a little olive oil. Preheat the oven to 375° F (180°C / Gas Mark 5).

2. Combine the tomatoes and garlic. Season with salt and pepper. Remove the basil leaves from the stems, chop the leaves and stir into the tomatoes. Slice the mozzarella and reserve a few slices.

3. For the béchamel sauce, melt the butter in a pan, stir in the flour and cook briefly. Add the milk gradually while stirring. Simmer until for about 10 minutes stirring continuously. Season with salt and pepper.

4 Spoon a little of the béchamel sauce on the bottom of the baking dish.

5. Place a layer of lasagna sheets on top, then some of the tomato mixture and another layer of lasagna. Add some more béchamel sauce, some mozzarella and a few basil leaves.

6. Continue layering until all the ingredients have been used. Finish with béchamel sauce and the reserved mozzarella.

7. Sprinkle with the hard cheese and season with salt and pepper.

8 Bake in the preheated oven for 40–45 minutes until golden brown.

Spinach Lasagne

Ingredients

2¼ lb / 1 kg fresh spinach, washed and sorted

12 sheets lasagna sheets, no precook type

1 onion, peeled and finely chopped

2 garlic cloves, peeled and finely chopped

1 tbsp butter, plus extra for greasing

Nutmeg

1 cup / 200 g cream cheese

²/₃ cup / 150 ml crème fraîche

½ cup / 60 g grated Emmental cheese

Butter, for greasing

Salt and freshly ground pepper

Method

Prep and cook time: 1 hour 10 min

1. Preheat the oven to 400°F (200°C / Gas Mark 6).

2. Blanch the spinach briefly in salted water, reserving a few leaves for the garnish. Drain, refresh, squeeze to remove any excess liquid and chop roughly.

3. Fry the onion and garlic in butter, add the spinach, remove from the heat and season with salt, pepper and nutmeg.

4. To make the cheese sauce, melt the cream cheese and crème fraîche in a heavy saucepan and season with salt and pepper.

5 Layer up the lasagna sheets, cheese sauce and spinach alternately in a buttered ovenproof dish, finishing with cheese sauce. Scatter with grated Emmental.

6. Bake for about 40 minutes until golden brown (cover with foil if it colors too quickly) and serve garnished with the reserved spinach leaves.

Lemon Risotto
with Herbs and Pine Nuts

Ingredients

4 cups / 1 liter chicken broth (stock)

1 onion, peeled and finely chopped

2 garlic cloves, peeled and finely chopped

3 tbsp olive oil

2 cups / 400 g risotto rice

1 cup / 250 ml dry white wine

1 lemon, juice and zest

1 tbsp chopped fresh parsley leaves

3 tbsp pine nuts

3 tbsp freshly grated hard cheese

1 tbsp butter

Lemon halves, for garnishing

Salt and freshly ground pepper

Method

Prep and cook time: 30 min

1. Heat the broth (stock) in a pan.

2. Sauté the onion and garlic in a skillet (frying pan) with 3 tbsp of hot oil.

3. Add the rice and sauté briefly. Pour in the wine. Bring the ingredients to a boil quickly then add the lemon juice and zest and a little hot broth.

4. Cook the risotto over medium heat, stirring constantly and adding more broth gradually as it is absorbed, until the rice is creamy but still firm (about 20 minutes).

5. Mix the parsley, pine nuts, hard cheese and butter into the risotto. Season to taste with salt and pepper. Garnish with the lemon halves and serve.

Baked Polenta Gnocchi

Ingredients

1¼ cups / 250 g quick-cooking polenta

For the sauce:

4 tbsp olive oil

1 onion, chopped

1 garlic clove, chopped

1 lb / 450 g ripe tomatoes

1 tbsp basil, shredded

2½ oz / 5 tbsp / 75 g butter

½ cup / 50 g freshly grated
hard cheese

Salt and freshly ground pepper

Method

Prep and cook time: 50 min

1. Prepare the polenta according to the package instructions.

2. Heat the olive oil and sweat the onion and garlic until soft.

3. Blanch the tomatoes briefly, refresh in cold water, then skin, quarter, de-seed and dice finely.

4. Add to the onion with salt and pepper and simmer for 2–3 minutes. Stir in the basil.

5. Preheat the oven to 375°F (200°C / Gas Mark 5).

6. Butter an ovenproof dish. Using a moistened tablespoon, cut gnocchi out of the polenta and arrange in the dish.

7. Pour the tomato sauce over, sprinkle with grated hard cheese and dot with the remaining butter.

8. Bake in the preheated oven for 25–30 minutes.

Linguine with Creamy Cep Mushrooms

Ingredients

14 oz / 400 g linguine

Good 1½ cups / 400 ml vegetable broth (stock)

2 tbsp / 10 g dried cep mushrooms

7 oz / 200 g fresh cep mushrooms

2 tbsp olive oil

1 onion

2 cloves garlic

2 tbsp chopped fresh parsley

3 tbsp crème fraîche

Salt & freshly milled pepper

Method

Prep and cook time: 40 min

1. Warm the vegetable broth (stock) and soak the dried cep mushrooms in the broth for about 20 minutes.

2. Clean the fresh cep mushrooms and cut into slices. Peel and finely chop the onion and the garlic.

3. Cook the linguine in boiling, salted water until al dente.

4. Fry the fresh mushrooms in hot oil over a high heat. Add the onions and garlic and sauté, then season with salt and pepper.

5. Pour the soaked mushrooms into a sieve and catch the liquid. If possible, strain the liquid through a filter to make it clear.

6. Rinse the soaked mushrooms, then add to the fried mushrooms in the skillet (frying pan) along with the strained liquid. Bring to a boil and simmer for 3 minutes.

7. Stir in the crème fraîche and the chopped parsley. Season to taste with salt and pepper. Drain the linguine and serve with the creamy cep mushroom sauce.

Tagliatelle with Lemon and Chili

Ingredients

1 lb 2 oz / 500 g tagliatelle

4 red chilies

2 oz / 50 g arugula (rocket) or spinach leaves

3–4 tbsp olive oil

1–2 unwaxed lemons

1 tbsp / 15 g butter

Salt & freshly milled pepper

Method

Prep and cook time: 25 min

1. Wash the lemons in hot water, then dry and grate the lemon zest. Cut one lemon in half and squeeze out the juice.

2. Cook the tagliatelle in boiling, salted water until al dente.

3. In the meantime, wash, deseed and finely chop the chilis. Wash the arugula (rocket) leaves, then leave to drain.

4. Melt the butter in a skillet, sauté the lemon zest, then add the chili and the olive oil. Season to taste with salt and lemon juice.

5. Drain the tagliatelle, then toss immediately in the lemon–butter sauce. Mix in the arugula leaves and serve on warmed plates. Sprinkle a little freshly milled pepper over the top before serving.

Herb Ravioli

Ingredients

For the dough:

3½ cups / 400 g Italian pasta flour

1–2 egg yolks

2 eggs

1 pinch Salt

1 tbsp safflower oil

For the filling:

7 oz / 200 g baking potatoes

1 slice stale white bread

2 oz / 4 tbsp / 50 g soft butter

1 shallot

1 bunch chives

1 bunch parsley

A few sprigs chervil

Scant ½ cup / 100 ml crème fraîche

Salt & freshly milled pepper

In addition:

flour, for the work surface

1 egg white

4 slices (rashers) smoked, streaky bacon

1 bunch chives

Chervil or parsley, to garnish

Method

Prep and cook time: 1 hour plus resting time 1 hour

1. Combine the flour, egg yolks, eggs, oil, salt and 2–3 tablespoons cold water and quickly knead to a pliable dough. Form into a ball, cover and let rest for 1 hour.

2. For the filling, peel and quarter the potatoes and cook in boiling, salted water for 20 minutes.

3. Finely dice the bread. Heat 1 tablespoon butter and fry the diced bread until golden brown to make croûtons. Let cool, then reserve 1 tablespoon of the croûtons for serving.

4. Peel the shallot and chop very finely. Wash the herbs, dry and chop very finely. Drain and mash the potatoes, let cool slightly, then mix with the rest of the butter, salt, pepper, herbs, croûtons and crème fraîche.

5. Divide the pasta dough in half and on a floured surface roll out thinly into 2 sheets. Put teaspoonfuls of the filling on one of the sheets of pasta, leaving about 2 inches / 6 cm between them. Brush the dough around the filling with egg white. Lay the second sheet of pasta dough on top and press together between the heaps of filling. Then cut out the ravioli with a pastry wheel.

6. Put the ravioli into boiling, salted water and cook for 4–5 minutes, then take out and keep warm. Dice the bacon and fry until crisp and brown. Wash the chives, shake dry and snip. Serve the ravioli onto warmed plates, scatter with bacon, chives and croûtons and serve garnished with chervil or parsley.

Creamy Mushrooms with Dumplings

Ingredients

For the dumplings:

1 shallot, finely chopped

1 tbsp butter

250 ml / 1 cup lukewarm milk

450 g / 1 lb stale white bread, crust removed

3 eggs

2 tbsp freshly chopped parsley

Salt and freshly ground pepper

For the mushroom sauce:

2 shallots, finely chopped

About 2 tbsp butter

200 ml / 7/8 cup dry white wine

250 ml / 1 cup cream, 30% fat

2 tbsp crème fraîche

2 tbsp freshly chopped parsley

1 tbsp snipped chives

450 g / 1 lb fresh wild mushrooms
Salt and freshly ground pepper

Method

Prep and cook time: 1 hour 10 min

1. For the dumplings, sweat the shallot in hot butter without coloring until translucent.

2. In a large bowl, pour the warm milk over the bread, add the eggs, parsley and shallot, season with salt and pepper and mix well. Leave to stand for about 20 minutes.

3. Form the dough into smooth round dumplings and simmer gently for about 20 minutes in salted water.

4. For the mushroom sauce, sweat the shallot briefly in hot butter, add the wine and reduce slightly. Add the cream and crème fraîche, simmer until slightly thickened and season with salt and pepper. Add the parsley and chives.

5. Thoroughly clean and rougly chop the mushrooms and fry them in hot butter for 3–4 minutes until golden brown and season with salt and pepper.

6. Arrange the mushrooms on plates, pour over the cream sauce, add the dumplings and serve garnished with parsley.

Bean Goulash

Ingredients

1 onion, finely chopped

2 garlic cloves, finely chopped

2 celery stalks, finely chopped

2 tbsp olive oil

1/2 tsp caraway

1 tbsp tomato paste (purée)

1 tbsp spicy ground paprika

2/3 cup /150 ml red wine

2½ cups / 600 ml vegetable broth (stock)

2 cups / 400 g canned tomatoes, chopped

2½ cups / 400 g canned kidney beans, rinsed and drained

2 red bell peppers, deseeded and finely chopped

1 red onion, finely chopped

Cayenne pepper

4 tbsp sour cream

Method

Prep and cook time: 40 min

1. Fry the onion, garlic and celery in hot oil.

2. Add the caraway, tomato paste (purée) and paprika and continue frying for a few minutes.

3. Add the red wine and reduce slightly. Add the vegetable broth (stock) and tomatoes and simmer gently for 20 minutes, stirring occasionally.

4. Push the mixture through a sieve, return to the pan and bring to a boil.

5. Add the beans, chopped peppers and chopped red onion and season to taste with salt and cayenne pepper.

6. Rest for a few minutes to allow the flavors to mingle, ladle into bowls and serve with a dollop of sour cream, garnished with parsley and a sprinkling of cayenne pepper.

Peppers
with Couscous, Pine Nuts and Raisins

Ingredients

8 medium red peppers halved lengthwise and seeded (stems intact)

1½ cups / 350 ml chicken broth (stock)

1 pinch saffron threads

½ cup / 100 g raisins

2 oz / ½ stick / 50 g butter

2 cloves garlic, minced

1 cup / 150 g couscous

1 tbsp curry powder

1½ tsp garam masala

1 cup / 80 g finely chopped toasted almonds

½ cup / 40 g toasted pine nuts

2 tsp finely chopped shallots

Salt and freshly ground pepper, to taste

8 small bay leaves, stalks attached

Melted butter for basting

For the chili yogurt sauce:

1 cup / 250 g plain yogurt

4 tbsp milk

Juice of ½ lemon

1 pinch chili powder

1 pinch cayenne pepper

½ tsp sweet paprika

Salt, to taste

Method

Prep and cook time: 1 h

1. Preheat the broiler (grill) at low setting.

2. Fill a large bowl with very cold water. Bring a large saucepan of water to a boil. Add the peppers and cook 2–3 minutes; quickly remove them with a slotted spoon to the water to cool. Drain and set aside.

3. Heat the broth (stock) in a saucepan until hot. Add the saffron threads, raisins, butter and garlic and stir briefly, then add the couscous and stir gently. Cover and let stand 30 minutes.

4. Fluff the couscous with a fork and season with curry powder, garam masala, almonds, pine nuts, shallots, salt and pepper.

5. Stuff the peppers with the couscous mixture, using the bay leaf stalks to hold the sides and secure the filling (or use toothpicks). Brush with melted butter and place under the broiler (grill) for about 15 minutes, turning the peppers frequently and brushing them with melted butter.

6. Meanwhile, prepare the yogurt sauce: combine the yogurt, milk, lemon juice, chili powder, cayenne pepper and paprika powder and season with salt.

7. Place the pepper halves onto plates, pour a little yogurt sauce over the top and serve.

Ratatouille

Ingredients

2 large zucchini (courgettes)

1 large eggplant (aubergine)

1 red bell pepper

1 yellow bell pepper

14 oz / 400 g tomatoes, fresh or canned

1 red onion

4 cloves garlic

3 sprigs fresh thyme

6 tbsp olive oil

Salt & freshly milled pepper

2 tbsp fresh basil, finely chopped

Method
Prep and cook time: 40 min

1. Wash and trim the zucchini (courgettes) and the eggplant (aubergine). Wash, trim, halve and de-seed the bell peppers.

2. Cut the prepared vegetables into small, bite-size cubes.

3. If using fresh tomatoes, drop them into boiling water for a few seconds, then immediately into cold water. Now skin the tomatoes, then quarter, de-seed and dice.

4. Peel and finely chop the garlic and the onion. Wash the thyme, shake dry and chop.

5. Heat 4 tablespoons of oil in a saucepan and fry the diced eggplant over a medium heat for about 2 minutes, stirring continually.

6. Add the zucchini, bell peppers, onion, garlic, thyme and the remaining oil and fry briefly.

7. Now add the tomatoes and season the vegetables to taste with salt and pepper. Cover and simmer over a low heat for about 15 minutes, stirring occasionally.

8. Season with salt and pepper and mix in the basil.

Stuffed Bell Peppers

Ingredients

4 red and yellow bell peppers

7 oz / 200 g sheep's milk cheese, chopped

16 red and yellow cherry tomatoes, halved

1 bunch basil, roughly chopped

Salt & freshly milled pepper

2 tbsp olive oil

2 tbsp lemon juice

1 lemon

Method
Prep and cook time: 20 min

1. Halve the bell peppers lengthways, remove the cores, and wash and dry the pepper halves.

2. Mix the cheese, tomatoes, and basil, season with salt and pepper, and stir in the oil and lemon juice. Stuff the bell pepper halves with the mixture and secure with toothpicks. Grill on a hot grill (on a piece of aluminum foil if necessary) for about 5 minutes.

3. Serve garnished with lemon wedges.

Vegetable Patties with Tomato Sauce

Ingredients

For the vegetable patties:

14 oz / 400 g cauliflower, chopped finely

1¼ lb / 600 g boiling (waxy) potatoes, peeled and grated

2 eggs

1 tbsp parsley, chopped

1–2 tbsp flour

Salt & freshly milled pepper

Nutmeg

Breadcrumbs, to coat

For the tomato sauce:

1 shallot, finely chopped

1 clove garlic, finely chopped

2 tbsp olive oil

1 tbsp tomato paste (purée)

14 oz / 400 g can chopped tomatoes

Salt & freshly milled black pepper

Method

Prep and cook time: 1 hour

1. To make the vegetable patties, mix the potatoes and cauliflower with the eggs, parsley and flour until combined and easy to form. Season to taste with salt, pepper, and nutmeg. Form the dough into small patties and roll in the breadcrumbs until coated.

2. For the tomato sauce: sauté the shallot and garlic in hot oil, then stir in the tomato paste (purée) and add the chopped tomatoes. Add a little water if required. Simmer gently for about 10 minutes. Purée with a hand blender and season with salt and pepper.

3. Place the vegetable patties under a hot broiler (grill) until golden brown, turning occasionally.

4. Arrange onto plates, drizzle tomato sauce over the top and serve.

Lentil Burgers with Yogurt Dip

Ingredients

1 cup / 200 g brown lentils

Some fresh thyme

1 bay leaf

1 stale wholegrain bread roll

1 onion

2 cloves garlic

3 tbsp sunflower oil

1 bunch parsley

1 chili

1 carrot

2 tbsp sesame seeds

Pinch ground cumin

Pinch ground coriander

Pinch ground nutmeg

Pinch cayenne pepper

1 egg

2 tbsp flour

For the yoghurt dip:

2 scallions (spring onions)

1 cup / 200 g plain yogurt

Salt

Method

Prep and cook time: 1 h 20 min

1. Rinse the lentils under running, cold water, then place in a large pan together with 4 cups (1 liter) of water, the thyme and bay leaf. Cover with a lid and cook for about 30–35 minutes until soft.

2. During the last 5 minutes of cooking, open the lid and cook on a high heat, stirring constantly until all the liquid has evaporated and the lentils are beginning to fall into pieces. Remove the thyme and the bay leaf.

3. Soak the bread in warm water. Peel and finely chop the onion and the garlic. Fry in 1 tablespoon of oil until golden, then season with salt.

4. Finely chop the parsley leaves. Add the chopped parsley to the onions and remove from the heat. Wash, halve, de-seed and finely chop the chili. Peel and grate the carrot. Squeeze the water out of the bread roll.

5. Mix the lentils with the chopped chili, salt, onion mix, bread, carrots, sesame seeds and spices and season to taste. Add the egg and the flour and form 8 flat patties. Brush with the remaining oil and fry gently for about 5 minutes on each side.

6. For the yogurt dip, wash and trim the scallions (spring onions) and cut into thin rings. Mix with the yogurt and season to taste with salt. Serve the burgers with the yogurt dip and salad.

Egg Fried Rice
with Onions and Mushrooms

Ingredients

3 tbsp vegetable oil

8 scallions (spring onions), sliced diagonally into rings (reserve a few for garnish)

8 oz / 250 g mushrooms, halved

1 1/3 cups / 250 g long-grain rice

6 eggs

Freshly ground pepper, to taste

2 tbsp light soy sauce, plus more to taste

Sliced scallion (spring onion), to garnish

Method

Prep and cook time: 40 min

1. Cook the rice according to the instructions on the package and let cool completely.

2. Heat the oil in a wok or skillet. Add the scallion (spring onion) rings and stir-fry for 2 minutes. Add the mushrooms and stir-fry until all liquid has evaporated.

3. Add the rice and cook, stirring, about 3 minutes, then push the rice mixture to the edges of the wok.

4. In a small bowl, whisk the eggs and season with pepper and 2 tbsp soy sauce. Pour into the center of the wok and cook quickly, stirring constantly. Lightly mix the eggs through the rice and season with soy sauce, to taste. Scatter with the reserved scallion rings and serve at once.

Stir-Fried Vegetables with Tofu

Ingredients

2 tsp vegetable oil, divided

1 lb / 450 g extra firm tofu, cut into cubes

4 shallots, quartered

2 cloves garlic, crushed

1 inch / 3 cm piece fresh ginger root, peeled and grated

7 oz / 200 g baby corn

8 oz / 225 g snow peas or sugar snap peas

8 oz / 225 g bean sprouts

8 oz / 225 g oyster and/or shiitake mushrooms, halved if large

1 cup / 225 ml vegetable broth (stock)

1 tbsp dark brown sugar

1 tbsp light soy sauce

2 tsp cornstarch (cornflour), mixed to a smooth paste in 2 tbsp of water

Method

Prep and cook time: 20 min

1. In a nonstick skillet (frying pan), heat 1 teaspoon of the oil over medium-high heat until hot. Add tofu and cook, gently tossing, for about 4 minutes until lightly golden. Transfer to a plate and set aside.

2. Meanwhile, heat the remaining teaspoon of oil in a large skillet or wok. Add the shallots, garlic, ginger, corn, snow peas, bean sprouts and mushrooms. Cook for 5 minutes, stirring frequently.

3. Add the tofu to the wok. Pour in the broth (stock), sugar, soy sauce and cornstarch (cornflour) mixture. Heat to boiling and cook for 2 minutes until the sauce thickens. Serve at once.

Vegetable Curry

Ingredients

3 cups / 600 g broccoli, cut into florets

2 cups / 300 g green beans

4 carrots

1 red bell pepper

2 cloves garlic

Oil

1–2 tbsp yellow curry paste,

1 can coconut milk

Chili, according to taste

Salt

Cilantro (coriander) sprigs

Method
Prep and cook time: 35 min

1. Wash the broccoli. Wash and trim the beans. Peel the carrots; cut into quarters lengthways, then into pieces. Wash, halve and de-seed the bell pepper and cut into strips. Peel the garlic and finely chop. Blanch the beans for 8 minutes in boiling, salted water, the carrots for 5 minutes and the broccoli florets for 4 minutes.

2. Drain the vegetables well.

3. Heat the curry paste with 1 tablespoon of oil in a skillet. Sauté the garlic, then pour in the coconut milk. Bring to a boil, then reduce the heat and add the bell pepper. Simmer for about 3 minutes.

4. Add the broccoli, green beans and carrots and simmer for a further 2–3 minutes. Season to taste with chili and salt.

5. Garnish the vegetable curry with fresh cilantro (coriander) sprigs and serve with rice.

Lentil Curry with Paneer

Ingredients

2 onions

2 cloves garlic

2 tbsp ghee or clarified butter

1 tsp curcuma (turmeric)

Pinch of ground cloves

Pinch of ground cumin

Pinch of ground allspice

2 curry leaves

1 cup /250 ml unsweetened coconut milk

1¾ cups / about 400 ml vegetable broth (stock)

1 cup / 200 g black lentils

1 cup / 200 g red lentils

Salt & freshly milled pepper

7 oz / 200 g paneer cheese

Method
Prep and cook time: 35 min

1. Peel and finely chop the onions and garlic. Heat the ghee (or clarified butter) and sauté the onions and garlic, add the spices and sauté briefly before pouring in the coconut milk. Stir in a little broth (stock) and the black lentils, cover and simmer gently for about 10 minutes.

2. Add the red lentils and a little more broth. Simmer for a further 10 minutes or so, stirring occasionally and add the rest of the broth (stock) as necessary.

3. Finally remove the curry leaves and season to taste with salt and pepper.

4. Dice the paneer and add to the curry. Serve with flatbread.

Vegetarian Cottage Pie

Ingredients

12 oz / 350 g floury potatoes

2 onions, finely chopped

2 tbsp vegetable oil

2 carrots, finely chopped

1 yellow bell pepper, deseeded and chopped

1 red bell pepper, deseeded and chopped

1 tbsp flour

1 cup / 250 ml vegetable broth (stock)

1 cup / 100 g frozen peas, thawed

1 cup / 200 g canned lentils, rinsed and drained

1/3 cup / 75 ml hot milk

Nutmeg

Butter, for greasing

1/2 cup / 50 g grated hard cheese

Method

Prep and cook time: 1 hour 30 min

1. Preheat the oven to 400°F (200°C / Gas Mark 6).

2. Cook the potatoes in boiling salted water for about 25 minutes until soft.

3. Sweat the onions in hot oil, add the carrots and bell peppers and continue frying.

4. Dust with the flour and add the vegetable broth (stock).

5. Stir in the peas and lentils and season with salt and pepper.

6. Drain and mash the potatoes, stir in the hot milk and season with salt, pepper and nutmeg.

7. Grease 4 individual pie dishes with butter.

8. Spoon the lentil mixture into the dishes, top with mashed potato and scatter with cheese.

9. Bake in the middle of the preheated oven for 30 minutes until golden brown.

Lentil Loaf

Ingredients

1 tbsp olive oil

2 tbsp sunflower seeds

1/2 cup / 100 g dry yellow lentils, rinsed

8 oz / 225 g floury potatoes, coarsely grated

2 onions, chopped

1 clove garlic, chopped

1 leek, chopped

4 oz / 100 g white turnips, chopped

2/3 cup / 100 g pistachio nuts, chopped

2–3 tbsp whole wheat flour

2 eggs

2 tbsp freshly chopped parsley

Nutmeg

Salt and freshly ground pepper

Method

Prep and cook time: 1 hour 30 min

1. Preheat the oven to 325°F (180°C / Gas Mark 3).

2. Grease a loaf pan with oil and scatter with sunflower seeds.

3. Place the lentils in a saucepan and cover with cold water. Bring to a boil, cover and simmer for about 30 minutes until cooked but not disintegrating. Drain and let cool.

4. If the potatoes are very wet, squeeze to remove excess liquid. Place in a mixing bowl.

5. Add the onions, garlic, leek, turnips, pistachios, flour, eggs, lentils and parsley to the potatoes and mix well.

6. Season the mixture with salt, pepper and nutmeg and turn into the loaf pan. Smooth the surface and bake for 40 minutes until golden brown.

Potato Soufflé

Ingredients

1¼ lb / 600 g potatoes

Butter, for greasing

8 oz / 225 g filo pastry

1 onion, peeled and finely chopped

2 oz / 4 tbsp / 50 g butter

½ cup / 100 g quark

4 sprigs fresh marjoram, leaves stripped and finely chopped

¾ cup / 75 g hard cheese

2 eggs, separated

Nutmeg

Salt and freshly ground pepper

4 sprigs fresh marjoram, to garnish

Method

Prep and cook time: 1 hour 30 min

1. Preheat the oven to 375°F (180°C / Gas Mark 5).

2. Cook the potatoes in salted boiling water for 30 minutes until soft. Drain, peel and press through a ricer. Leave to steam dry and cool slightly.

3. Grease 4 ramekins with butter.

4. Lay out the filo pastry in double layers and cut out squares about 15x15 cm/6x6 inch. Line the ramekins with the pastry and brush with melted butter.

5. Fry the onion in hot butter until translucent and let cool slightly.

6. Mix the quark with the chopped marjoram, two thirds of the hard cheese, the egg yolks, onion and potatoes.

7. Beat the egg whites until stiff, then fold carefully into the potato mixture and season to taste with salt, pepper and nutmeg.

8. Spoon into the ramekins and scatter with the remaining cheese.

9. Bake for about 25 minutes in the middle of the preheated oven until golden brown.

10. Garnish with the remaining marjoram sprigs and serve.

Spinach Quiche

Ingredients

For the pastry:

2 cups / 200 g all-purpose (plain) flour

¼ tsp salt

3½ oz / 7 tbsp /100 g cold butter, chopped, plus extra butter for greasing

1 egg

For the filling:

2 tbsp butter

1 leek, finely chopped

2 garlic cloves, finely chopped

1¾ cups / 400 g cream cheese

3 eggs

1 cup / 250 ml whipping cream

1 cup / 100 g freshly grated hard cheese

1 lb / 450 g young spinach, rinsed and roughly chopped

Nutmeg

Salt and freshly ground pepper

Method

Prep and cook time: 1 hour

1. Heat the oven to 400°F (200°C / Gas Mark 6).

2. Pour the flour onto a work surface in a heap and add the salt. Make a well in the middle and scatter with the butter.

3. Crack the egg into the well, add 2–3 tbsp of lukewarm water and cut all ingredients together with a knife to form a crumbly consistency.

4. Using your hands, knead quickly to a dough, form into a ball, wrap in plastic wrap and chill for around 30 minutes.

5. To make the filling, melt the butter in a pan and gently fry the leek and garlic until soft.

6. Mix the cream cheese with the eggs, cream and half the hard cheese to a smooth consistency.

7. Add the spinach, garlic and leek and season with salt, pepper and nutmeg.

8. Roll the pastry out between two sheets of plastic wrap; use to line a tart pan 10 inches / 26 cm in diameter

9. Pour the filling into the pastry case and smooth the surface. Sprinkle with the remaining hard cheese and bake for around 40 minutes until golden brown.

Cherry Tomato and Basil Tart

Ingredients

2 cups / 400 g ricotta cheese

2 eggs

7 tbsp milk

⅔ cup / 60 g freshly grated hard cheese

Some sprigs fresh basil, leaves plucked

2 tbsp pine nuts

1 garlic clove

Olive oil

12 oz / 300 g filo pastry

1 lb / 450 g cherry tomatoes, halved

1 tsp brown sugar

2 tbsp lemon juice

Salt and freshly ground pepper

Method

Prep and cook time: 1 hour

1. Heat the oven to 425°F (220° C / Gas Mark 7.)

2. Mix together the ricotta, eggs, milk and hard cheese and season with salt and pepper.

3. Purée two thirds of the basil leaves to a paste with the pine nuts, garlic and about 5 tbsp olive oil.

4. Grease a baking pan (about 8 × 8 inches / 20 cm × 20 cm) with oil and line with several layers of filo pastry.

5. Spread the pastry base with about two thirds of the pesto and then spread the cheese mixture on top.

6. Toss the tomatoes with the sugar and lemon juice and season with salt and pepper.

7. Arrange the tomatoes on top of the cheese mixture, dot with the remaining pesto and drizzle with a little olive oil.

8. Bake for 35–40 minutes until golden brown. Scatter with the remaining basil leaves 5 minutes before the end of baking time.

9. Remove from the baking pan, cool on a wire rack and serve either warm or cold cut into slices.

Pancakes with Spinach, Mozzarella and Pine Nuts

Ingredients

For the batter:

1½ / 150 g cups flour

3 eggs

½ cup / 125 ml milk

½ cup / 125 ml sparkling mineral water

2 tbsp melted butter

Salt

Butter, for frying

For the filling:

1 tbsp butter

1 lb / 450 g fresh spinach, rinsed

2 garlic cloves, finely sliced

8 oz / 250 g mozzarella cheese, drained and sliced

½ cup / 50 g pine nuts, toasted without fat

Garnish:

Cherry tomatoes

Fresh herbs, e.g. sage, tarragon

Method

Prep and cook time: 1 hour

1. Heat the oven to 400°F (200°C / Gas Mark 6).

2. To make the batter, beat together all the ingredients and rest for 20 minutes. If the batter is too thick, add a little more water.

3. Heat a little butter in a skillet (frying pan) and make 8–12 thin pancakes from the batter. Set aside and keep warm.

4. To make the filling, melt the butter in a clean pan and fry the spinach and garlic until the spinach has wilted.

5. Divide the spinach between the pancakes, top with the cheese and fold the pancakes into quarters.

6. Place the pancakes on a cookie sheet lined with baking parchment, cover with foil and bake in the oven for about 5 minutes, until the cheese has melted.

7. Arrange the pancakes on a warmed plate and serve garnished with tomatoes and herbs.

Cheese and Vegetable Pie

Ingredients

1 lb / 450 g puff pastry, thawed if frozen

2 tbsp olive oil, plus extra for greasing

½ cup / 50 g freshly grated hard cheese

4 tomatoes, rinsed, cored and chopped or 1 cup / 200 g chopped canned tomatoes

1 lb / 450 g pumpkin flesh, peeled and chopped

1 lb / 450 g floury potatoes, peeled and chopped

2 zucchini (courgettes), rinsed, cleaned and sliced

1 onion, finely chopped

2 garlic cloves, finely chopped

½ cup / 50 g black olives, pitted and sliced

1 tsp dried thyme

4 tbsp white bread crumbs

8 oz / 225 g feta cheese

5 oz / 150 g mozzarella cheese, sliced

2 tbsp freshly chopped parsley

Salt and freshly ground pepper

Lettuce leaves, to serve

Method

Prep and cook time: 1 h 20 min

1. Heat the oven to 375°F (180° C / Gas Mark 5).

2. Roll out the pastry and cut out two circles for a pie dish 26 cm / 10 inches in diameter. Use one for the base and one for the lid of the pie.

3. Grease the pie dish with oil, line with pastry and scatter with a third of the hard cheese.

4. In a large bowl mix together the tomatoes, pumpkin, potatoes, zucchini (courgettes), onion, garlic, olives, thyme, olive oil, remaining cheese and bread crumbs and season with salt and pepper.

5. Spoon the filling into the pie dish and scatter with crumbled feta.

6. Moisten the edge of the pastry case, place the lid on top and press to seal.

7. Top the pastry with the mozzarella slices and bake for around 40 minutes, covering with foil if it browns too quickly.

8. Remove from the oven, cut into slices, scatter with parsley and serve with lettuce leaves if desired.

Baked Fish
with Vegetables

Ingredients

1lb 12 oz / 800 g white fish fillets, such as sole or monkfish

6 bell peppers, red, yellow and green

4 shallots

2 cloves garlic

3 tbsp olive oil

1 tbsp tomato paste (purée)

1 cup / 250 ml white wine

paprika, sweet

sea salt & milled pepper

2 balls of mozzarella cheese, cut into slices

some fresh thyme leaves and sprigs

cayenne pepper

Method

Prep and cook time: 45 min

1. Heat the oven to 350°F (180°C / Gas Mark 4).

2. Wash the fish fillets and pat dry. Cut into large even-sized pieces.

3. Wash and de-seed the bell peppers and chop into thin slices. Peel and finely chop the shallots and the garlic.

4. Sauté the shallots, garlic and the bell peppers in hot oil in a flameproof oven dish. Add the tomato purée and pour in the white wine.

5. Remove from the heat and put the fish fillets on the top. Season with paprika, sea salt and pepper and cover with sliced mozzarella. Sprinkle a few thyme leaves over the top.

6. Bake in the oven until cooked (about 20 minutes). Add a little water if needed.

7. Season to taste with sea salt and pepper; sprinkle the remaining thyme sprigs over the top and serve.

Fish Lasagna
with Capers and Cherry Tomatoes

Ingredients

Approx 9 lasagna sheets
(no pre-cook type)

2 cloves garlic

2 red onions

4 tbsp olive oil

1 can chopped tomatoes
(about 14 oz / 400 g)

½ cup / 100 g tomato paste (purée)

½ cup / 100 g capers

1 lb 12 oz / 800 g white fish fillets

1 tbsp lemon juice

1 bunch dill weed (dill)

2½ cups / 400 g cherry tomatoes

Salt & freshly milled pepper

1 cup / 100 g grated cheese

Method

Prep and cook time: 1 hour

1. Heat the oven to 350°F (180°C / Gas Mark 4).

2. Soak the lasagna in plenty of cold water for 10 minutes.

3. Peel and finely chop the garlic and onions. Heat 1 tablespoon oil and sauté the garlic and onions. Add the canned tomatoes, tomato paste (purée) and capers and simmer for about 20 minutes until reduced.

4. Wash and dry the fish fillets, sprinkle with lemon juice and cut into long strips about ¾ inch (2 cm) wide. Heat the remaining oil and quickly sauté the fish. Take out of the skillet and put on a large plate.

5. Finely chop the dill weed. Wash and halve the cherry tomatoes. Remove the tomato sauce from the heat and stir in the cherry tomatoes and dill weed. Season with salt and pepper.

6. Now fill a baking dish with alternate layers of lasagna, tomato sauce and fish, finishing with tomato sauce. Sprinkle with grated cheese and bake in the oven for 20–25 minutes.

Fish Stew with Crème Fraîche

Ingredients

1 lb 6 oz / 600 g fish fillet, eg bass or monkfish

2 carrots,

1 clove garlic

2 shallots

1 bunch scallions (spring onions)

2 tbsp / 25 g butter

1 tbsp flour

¾–1 cup / 200 ml white wine

¾–1 cup / 200 ml fish broth (stock)

Good ½ cup / 125 g crème fraîche

1 bunch dill weed

Lemon juice

Salt & white pepper

Method

Prep and cook time: 30 min

1. Wash, dry and dice the fish fillet.

2. Peel the carrots, garlic and shallots. Slice the carrots and finely dice the garlic and shallots. Wash and trim the scallions (spring onions) and cut into 1 inch (3 cm) lengths.

3. Heat the butter in a frying pan and sauté the carrots, garlic and shallots. Dust with flour and stir in the white wine. Simmer until reduced slightly, then add the fish broth (stock).

4. Stir in the crème fraîche and simmer gently for 5–6 minutes. Then add the fish and scallions and cook over a low heat for a further 6–8 minutes, until done.

5. Chop the dill weed (reserving a few sprigs to garnish) and mix into the stew.

6. Season to taste with a few drops of lemon juice, salt and pepper and serve garnished with the reserved dill weed.

Baked Cod with Mash and Leeks

Ingredients

1¼ lb / 500 g floury potatoes, peeled

2 tbsp olive oil

1 red onion, chopped

2 tomatoes, deseeded and chopped

3 tbsp bread crumbs

3 tbsp freshly grated Parmesan cheese

2 tbsp thinly sliced basil leaves

5 tbsp butter

2 leeks, finely sliced

1/3 cup / 75 ml milk

¼ tsp nutmeg

4 cod fillets, about 150 g / 5 oz each

2–3 tbsp lime juice

1 tbsp vegetable oil

Salt and freshly ground pepper

Method

Prep and cook time: 1 hour

1. Put the peeled potatoes in a pan. Cover with salted water. Bring to a boil and cook until tender.

2. Heat the olive oil in a pan and cook the onion until transparent. Add the tomatoes and cook for a further 5 minutes.

3. Remove the onions and tomatoes from the pan and mix with the bread crumbs, Parmesan cheese and basil leaves. Season to taste with salt and pepper and set aside.

4. Heat 2 tbsp of the butter and sauté the sliced leeks.

5. Drain the potatoes, return to the pan and add the milk. Mash until smooth then season with salt, pepper and the nutmeg. Stir in the leeks.

6. Turn the broiler (grill) on to its highest setting

7. Season the cod fillets with the lime juice, salt and pepper. Heat the remaining butter and the vegetable oil in a pan and gently fry the fillets for 2–3 minutes on each side.

8. Place the fish fillets in a lightly buttered casserole dish. Cover with the tomato mixture, place on the top oven rack and broil for about 2 minutes.

9. Divide the mashed potatoes and leeks and cod fillets au gratin among 4 warmed plates.

Plaice Rolls with Orange Butter

Ingredients

4 sprigs thyme

4 garlic cloves

3 tbsp lemon juice

8 plaice or sole fillets, about
75 g / 3 oz each

1 tsp cayenne pepper

¼ tsp nutmeg

¼ tsp ground cloves

2 oranges

2½ oz / 5 tbsp / 75 g butter, plus
extra to grease the dish

1 tsp sugar

2 tbsp orange liqueur

1 tbsp orange marmalade

Salt and freshly ground pepper

Method

Prep and cook time: 45 min

1. Preheat the oven to 425° F (220°C / Gas Mark 7).

2. Wash the thyme and shake dry. Remove the leaves from the stem and finely chop them.

3. Peel the garlic cloves and crush them with a little salt.

4. Put the garlic and chopped thyme into a dish. Add the lemon juice, mix and allow to marinate.

5. Blot the plaice fillets dry. Sprinkle with pepper, cayenne pepper, nutmeg and cloves. Divide the thyme mixture evenly among the fillets.

6. Roll up the fillets and secure them with a wooden skewer or tooth pick. Place the fillets next to each other in a lightly greased ovenproof dish.

7. Squeeze the juice from one orange. Pour the juice evenly over the rolled fillets.

8. Cover with foil and cook in the preheated oven for about 15 minutes.

9. Wash the remaining orange in warm water and rub dry. Zest the orange and squeeze out the juice.

10. Melt the butter in a saucepan. Add the orange zest, sprinkle with sugar and allow it caramelize a little. Season to taste with the orange liqueur, marmalade and a little salt and pepper.

11. Remove the rolled fillets from the oven and place on warmed plates. Sprinkle with the orange zest, drizzle the sauce over the fillets and serve immediately.

Linguine
with Salmon and Cheese-Chive Sauce

Ingredients

14 oz / 400 g linguine

2 tbsp butter, divided

1 onion, finely diced

2 cloves garlic, minced

Scant ½ cup / 100 ml dry white wine

½ cup / 125 ml vegetable broth (stock)

1¼ cups / 150 g grated Gruyère cheese

⅔ cup / 150 g crème fraîche

Salt & freshly ground pepper, to taste

1 hot red chili pepper

1 lb / 450 g salmon fillet, skinned and cut into bite-size chunks

3 tbsp lemon juice

2 tbsp snipped chives

Method

Prep and cook time: 30 min

1. Cook the pasta in boiling salted water until al dente; drain and keep warm.

2. Meanwhile prepare the sauce: heat 1 tablespoon of the butter in a skillet; add onion and garlic and sauté until soft. Add the wine and broth (stock), then stir in the cheese and crème fraîche and simmer for about 5 minutes. Season with salt and pepper and set aside, keeping warm.

3. Wearing gloves to prevent irritation, seed and devein the chili and slice into thin strips. Heat the remaining butter in a skillet and fry the salmon and chili for 2–3 minutes. Season with salt, pepper and lemon juice.

4. Stir the chives into the sauce, toss with the drained pasta and arrange on plates, topped with the salmon.

Gingered Spaghetti
with Shrimps and Peas

Ingredients

14 oz / 400 g spaghetti

1½ cups / 400 g shrimp (prawns)

2 tbsp lemon juice

1¼ cups / 200 g frozen peas

2 thin leeks

2 cloves garlic

1 piece fresh root ginger, walnut size

2 tbsp olive oil

Scant ½ cup / 100 ml fish broth (stock)

Some cilantro (fresh coriander)

Method

Prep and cook time: 25 min

1. Wash the shrimps (prawns), then drain, place in bowl and drizzle lemon juice over the top.

2. Wash and trim the leeks and finely cut. Peel the garlic and the ginger and finely chop.

3. Heat the oil in a skillet, then sauté the garlic followed by the ginger. Now add the peas and the leeks and sauté. Pour in the fish broth (stock), cover and simmer for about 5 minutes over a medium heat.

4. Cook the spaghetti in boiling, salted water until al dente, then drain.

5. Wash the cilantro (coriander) and shake dry. Put a few leaves on the side and finely chop the rest.

6. Put the shrimps and the chopped cilantro into the sauce and simmer for a few minutes minutes. Toss the spaghetti in the sauce and serve immediately in warmed bowls. Garnish with the remaining cilantro sprigs.

Fish Pie

Ingredients

1 lb 10 oz / 800 g russet or other starchy potato, peeled and cut into chunks

8 oz / 250 g skinless white fish fillet

8 oz / 250 g skinless smoked haddock fillet

2½ cups / 600 ml full-fat milk, divided

1 small onion, quartered

8 oz / 200 g frozen peas

3½ oz / 7 tbsp / 100 g butter, divided

½ cup / 50 g all-purpose (plain) flour

Salt and freshly ground pepper, to taste

Pinch freshly grated nutmeg

Method

Prep and cook time: 1 hour 15 min

1. Put the potatoes into a large pan of salted water and bring to a boil. Reduce heat and simmer for 20 minutes until tender.

2. Meanwhile, arrange the white fish, smoked haddock and onion in a large skillet; add 2 cups / 475 ml of the milk. Bring the milk just to a boil – you will see a few small bubbles. Reduce the heat and simmer for 8 minutes; set aside.

3. Lift the fish into an ovenproof dish. Flake the fish into large pieces in the baking dish. Remove the onion and discard. Scatter the frozen peas over the fish.

4. To make the sauce, melt 3 tbsp of the butter in a saucepan; stir in the flour and cook for 1 minute over moderate heat. Gradually pour in a little of the poaching milk, then stir until blended. Continue to add the milk gradually, mixing well until you have a smooth thickened sauce. Remove from the heat, season with salt, pepper and nutmeg, then pour over the fish.

5. Heat oven to 400°F (200°C / Gas Mark 6).

6. Drain the potatoes and return to the pan with the remaining butter and milk. Season to taste and mash until smooth and lump free. Spoon the mashed potato all over the fish. Fluff the top with a fork.

7. Bake for 30 minutes until the top is golden.

Fish Cakes

Ingredients

1 lb / 450 g floury potatoes

3 tbsp milk

2 lb / 900 g pollock or cod fillet, skinned

1 tsp peppercorns

1 tbsp capers

Juice of 1 small lemon

2 tbsp chopped fresh dill

2 tbsp mayonnaise

Salt and pepper

3 tbsp all-purpose (plain) flour

Sunflower oil, for shallow frying

Sprigs of fresh dill, to garnish

Method

Prep and cook time: 35 min plus 30 min chilling

1. Peel the potatoes, cut into large chunks and put in a saucepan of salted water. Cover, bring to the boil and simmer for about 20 minutes, until tender. Drain, return to the pan and add the milk. Mash until smooth. Let cool.

2. Put the fish into a wide saucepan, cover with cold, salted water and add the peppercorns. Bring to the boil and simmer for 5–7 minutes, or until the fish is opaque and flakes easily. Using a slotted spoon, lift the fish from the liquid and put into a bowl.

3. Roughly chop the capers. Add the capers, lemon juice, dill, mayonnaise and mashed potato to the fish. Season with salt and pepper and mix well together.

4. Dust a work surface with the flour and form the mixture into 8 fish cakes. Chill in the refrigerator for 30 minutes.

5. Heat the oil in a large skillet (frying pan), add the fish cakes and fry for 2–3 minutes on each side, turning once, until golden brown. Serve the fish cakes with warm Hollandaise Sauce and garnish with fresh dill.

Tuna Salad
with Baked Tomatoes

Ingredients

1 ¼ lb / 600 g small ripe tomatoes, cored and halved horizontally

2 red onions, sliced into wedges

1 dried red chili pepper, seeded and finely chopped (wear gloves to prevent irritation)

Handful finely chopped mixed fresh herbs (try parsley, lemon balm, oregano, rosemary, sage and/or thyme)

5 tbsp olive oil, divided

Salt and freshly ground pepper, to taste

2 (6-oz / 200 g) cans water-packed tuna, drained and flaked

1 bunch arugula (rocket) leaves, trimmed

4 tbsp balsamic vinegar

Method

Prep and cook time: 30 min

1. Place an oven rack 5 inches from the heat; preheat the oven to 500°F (250°C / Gas Mark 9) Line a baking sheet with parchment or foil.

2. Place the tomatoes and onions cut-side-up on the baking sheet. In a small bowl, combine the chili, herbs, and half of the oil. Season with salt and pepper. Sprinkle over the tomatoes and bake until browned, 7–10 minutes.

3. In a small bowl or jar, mix the rest of the oil with the vinegar and season lightly with salt and pepper.

4. Put a bed of arugula (rocket) on each plate. Top with the tuna, tomatoes and onions and serve, sprinkled with the dressing.

Seafood Kebabs

Ingredients

4 large shrimp (prawns), peeled, deveined and halved

8 slices bacon

12 medium scallops

1 lemon, cut into quarters

16 medium shrimp (prawns)

1 lime, cut into eighths

Salt and freshly ground pepper, to taste

Cilantro (coriander) leaves, for garnish

Lemon-flavored oil and/or soy sauce, for dipping

Method

Prep and cook time: 30 min

1. Soak 8 wooden skewers in enough water to cover them for 15 minutes (to prevent burning). Preheat the broiler (grill).

2. Wrap each large shrimp with 2 slices of bacon. Thread 2 large bacon-wrapped shrimp, 3 scallops and a lemon quarter onto each of 4 skewers. Take the remaining 4 skewers and alternately thread the medium shrimp and the lime wedges onto each. Season the skewers with salt and pepper.

3. Broil (grill) for **about** 4 minutes on each side until the shrimp are golden brown. **Garnish** with cilantro (coriander) and serve with lemon oil and/or soy sauce.

Salmon
with Herbs and Lemon

Ingredients

1 whole salmon fillet, with skin

Salt, to taste

1 lemon

Scant ¼ cup / 50 ml olive oil

1 small onion, finely chopped

½ bunch parsley, finely chopped

½ bunch basil, finely chopped

⅓ bunch dill, finely chopped

½ inch / 1-cm piece fresh ginger root, peeled and minced

1–2 cloves garlic, minced

Freshly ground pepper, to taste

1 tsp sea salt

Method

Prep and cook time: 30 min

1. Preheat the oven to 400°F (200°C / Gas Mark 6). Grease a long, shallow baking dish (large enough to hold the salmon in a single layer).

2. Lightly salt the salmon. Using a zester or vegetable peeler, zest the lemon and slice into thin slivers. Halve, then juice the lemon into a medium bowl. Add the oil, onion, parsley, basil, dill, ginger, garlic, lemon zest, and pepper.

3. Place the salmon in the baking dish and cover with the lemon-herb mixture. Season with the sea salt. Bake for about 15 minutes or until firm. Serve immediately.

Fish Crumble

Ingredients

1 lb / 450 g fish fillet, cut into chunks

4 oz / 100 g medium shrimp (prawns)

8 oz / 250 g mascarpone

1 lemon

For the crumble:

Generous 1 cup / 125 g all-purpose (plain) flour

2½ oz / 5 tbsp / 75 g butter, cubed

1 tbsp chopped parsley,

Method

Prep and cook time: 55 min

1. Heat the oven to 375°F (190°C / Gas Mark 5). Grease a large baking dish.

2. Arrange the fish and shrimp in the dish.

3. Combine the mascarpone with 4 tbsp of cold water and the finely grated zest and juice of the lemon. Spoon the mascarpone mixture over the fish.

4. Put the flour, butter and parsley together in a food processor, or into a bowl. Pulse together in the processor, or rub together with your fingertips until the mixture forms crumbs.

5. Sprinkle the crumble mixture evenly over the fish. Bake for 35 minutes, until the crumble is golden.

Cod
with Potatoes, Olives and Tomatoes

Ingredients

1½ lb / 675 g new potatoes

1 onion, chopped

⅔ cup / 150 ml vegetable broth (stock)

1½ lb / 675 g cod fillets

1 lb / 450 g cherry tomatoes

1 cup / 80 g black olives, pitted

Juice of 1 lemon

2 tbsp olive oil

1 tbsp chopped fresh parsley leaves

Salt and freshly ground pepper

Method

Prep and cook time: 45 min

1. Preheat the oven to 355°F (180°C / Gas Mark 4).

2. Thoroughly wash and slice the potatoes. Place in a heat-resistant baking dish with the chopped onion.

3. Pour the vegetable broth (stock) over the top. Season with salt and pepper. Bake in the oven for about 15 minutes.

4. Rinse the cod fillets, pat dry and cut into large pieces.

5. Remove the dish from the oven, add the tomatoes, fish and olives and season with salt and pepper. Drizzle with the lemon juice and olive oil.

6. Continue cooking for another 15 minutes (add a little water if necessary). Garnish with parsley and serve.

Fried Noodles with Shrimp

Ingredients

14 oz / 400 g noodles

14 oz / 400 g shrimp (prawns), peeled
and deveined

1 cup / 200 g broccoli florets

1 red bell pepper, halved, cored and cut
into strips

1¾ cups / 200 g sugar snap peas,
trimmed

2 scallions (spring onions),
cut into rings

2 cloves garlic, peeled and finely chopped

1 chili, deseeded and finely chopped

3 tbsp sesame oil

1 tbsp sesame seeds

Fish sauce

Method

Prep and cook time: 30 min

1. Cook the noodles in boiling, salted water until al dente, then drain, refresh in cold water and drain well. Keep warm.

2. Wash and dry the shrimp (prawns).

3. Heat the oil and sauté the sugar snap peas, bell pepper, garlic, sesame seeds and chili. Then add the rest of the vegetables and stir-fry for 3–4 minutes. Add the noodles and shrimp and stir-fry for a further 2–3 minutes, until all the ingredients are cooked but still have a little bite. Season well with fish sauce and serve.

Tuna with Rice Noodle Salad

Ingredients

6 oz / 175 g thin rice noodles

2 tsp sesame oil

1 red bell pepper

6 scallions (spring onions)

2 tbsp soy sauce

1 tbsp chili sauce

1 tsp lime zest

4 tbsp lime juice

1 tbsp runny honey

5 tbsp olive oil

Salt

3 tbsp sesame seeds

4 tuna steaks, each weighing about
175 g/6 oz

4 tbsp vegetable oil

1 tsp coarsely ground mixed colored
(coloured) peppercorns

Method

Prep and cook time: 30 min plus 30 soaking

1. Put the rice noodles in a bowl of warm water and let soak for 30 minutes to soften. Drain well, put in a bowl and stir in a little of the sesame oil.

2. Thinly slice the red peppers, discarding the core and seeds. Thinly slice the scallions (spring onions).

3. Put the soy sauce, chili sauce, lime zest and juice, honey, remaining sesame oil and 3 tbsp of the olive oil in a large bowl and mix together. Season with salt.

4. Toast the sesame seeds in a dry non-stick skillet (frying pan). Remove from the pan and let cool.

5. Heat the remaining olive oil in the pan, add the red peppers and fry for 3-4 minutes. Add the scallions and fry for a further 2 minutes. Season with salt. Add the hot vegetables to the dressing. Add the toasted sesame seeds and mix together.

6. Season the tuna steaks with salt and pepper. Heat the vegetable oil in the pan and fry the steaks on each side for 2–3 minutes.

7. Serve the tuna topped with the noodles and salad and sprinkle with coarsely ground pepper.

Shrimp and Mango Curry

Ingredients

1 lb 2 oz / 500 g large shrimp
or prawns

2 mangoes

3 tbsp grated coconut

3 tbsp coconut milk

A good pinch of chili powder

2 tbsp curry powder

1 carrot

3 cloves garlic

2 onions

2 stalks celery, with leaves

2 tbsp sesame oil

Juice of ½ lemon

Salt & freshly milled pepper

Method

Prep and cook time: 30 min

1. Thaw the shrimp (prawns) in a sieve if frozen, moving them around frequently. Then pat dry.

2. Peel the mangoes and cut the flesh away from the stone in slices about ¼ inch / 5mm thick.

3. Put half the mango flesh into a blender with the grated coconut, coconut milk, chili powder, curry powder and 3 tablespoons of water and blend to a fine purée.

4. Peel the carrot, onions and garlic and dice very finely. Trim and wash the celery and dice finely. Reserve a few celery leaves.

5. Heat the sesame oil and briefly sauté the diced vegetables. Add the shrimp and sauté briefly. Stir in the puréed mango sauce and simmer gently for about 8 minutes. If the sauce becomes too thick, thin with a little coconut milk or warm water.

6. Season the seafood curry with lemon juice, sesame oil, salt and pepper. Serve garnished with the remaining mango slices and celery leaves.

Paella

Ingredients

About 2 lb / 1 kg of mixed skinless and boneless chicken

9 oz / 250 g shrimp (prawns), peeled and ready to cook

1 lb 12 oz / 800 g shellfish, (e.g. mussels)

2 tomatoes

2 red bell peppers, cut into strips

6 tbsp olive oil

1 onion, finely diced

1 clove garlic, finely diced

Scant 1 cup / 100 g frozen peas

Salt & freshly milled pepper

1 cup / 200 g paella rice

1¾ cups / 400 ml chicken broth (stock)

1 bay leaf

4 saffron threads

Method

Prep and cook time: 1 hour

1. Wash and dry the chicken with paper towel. Remove from the bone and cut into bite-size pieces.

2. Drop the tomatoes into boiling water for a few seconds, then skin, quarter, de-seed and chop.

3. Wash the shrimp (prawns), scrub the shellfish, scrape off the 'beards' from the mussels. Discard any shells that do not close when tapped.

4. Heat the oil in a large skillet or paella pan and slowly sauté the chicken on all sides until golden brown. Add the onion and fry briefly. Add the chopped garlic, bell peppers, tomatoes and peas and fry briefly. Season with salt and pepper.

5. Scatter the rice into the skillet and stir in carefully. Add the broth (stock), bay leaf and the saffron dissolved in a little water. You should not stir the paella again. Turn down the heat and simmer without a lid for 25–30 minutes.

6. About 10 minutes before the end of cooking time add the seafood. When cooked, discard any shells that remain closed. Check the seasoning and serve. The liquid should have been absorbed.

Kedgeree

Ingredients

2 tbsp vegetable oil

1 small onion, chopped

½ tsp garam masala*

1¼ cups / 300 g long-grain rice

2½ cups / 600 ml fish broth (stock)

½ bunch scallions (spring onions), chopped

12 oz / 300g smoked haddock, flaked

Salt and freshly ground pepper, to taste

2 oz / ½ stick / 50 g butter, melted

2–3 hard boiled eggs, chopped

4 tbsp chopped fresh parsley

Lemon juice, to taste

Lemon wedges, to garnish

Method

Prep and cook time: 35 min

1. Heat the oil in a large skillet; add the onion and garam masala and sauté until the onion is translucent. Add the rice and continue to sauté for about 1 minute, until the rice grains are well coated. Pour in the fish broth (stock) and bring to a boil; cover and simmer for about 20 minutes or until the rice has absorbed the liquid. Add the scallions (spring onions) and fish about 5 minutes before the end of cooking time.

2. Stir in the butter, chopped eggs and parsley; cook, stirring gently over medium heat for 1–2 minutes. Season to taste with lemon juice, garnish with a few lemon wedges and serve.

*Garam masala, a "warming" spice blend used in Indian cuisine, often contains black pepper, cinnamon, cloves, coriander, cumin, cardamom, fennel and other spices. Find it in Asian groceries and gourmet shops.

CAKES, BAKES AND DESSERTS

Scottish Dundee Cake

Ingredients

1–1¼ cup / 180 g golden raisins (sultanas)

4 oz / 125 g finely chopped figs

1–1¼ cup /180 g currants

Grated zest of 1 lemon

3 tbsp whiskey

6–8 candied cherries, quartered

2 oz / 50 g candied lemon peel,
finely chopped

2 oz / 50 g candied orange peel,
finely chopped

2½ cups / 250 g all-purpose (plain) flour

1½ tsp baking powder

6 oz / 1½ sticks /180 g butter

²/₃ cup / 125 g sugar

1 tbsp honey

3 large eggs

¹/₃ cup / 75 ml milk

Blanched almonds, for decorating

Confectioners' (icing) sugar for dusting

Marzipan (optional), for covering

Method

Prep and cook time 2 hours 30 min

1. Preheat the oven to 180°C (350°F / Gas Mark 4). Grease and line a 10 inch (26 cm) spring-release cake pan (tin).

2. Mix the raisins (sultanas), figs and currants with the lemon zest, whiskey and candied fruits in a large bowl and leave to stand.

3. Meanwhile, sift the flour and baking powder together. Cream the butter with the sugar and honey until light and fluffy. Gradually beat in the eggs and then beat in the flour, milk and soaked dried fruit. Turn the batter into the prepared cake pan and smooth the top. Decorate the top of the cake with the whole almonds.

4. Bake in the oven for 30 minutes, then reduce the oven temperature to 150°C (300°F / Gas Mark 2) and bake for a further 90 minutes. Cover the top with baking parchment if it browns too quickly. Cool in the pan for 15 minutes then take out and leave to cool completely.

5. Before serving, dust with confectioners' (icing) sugar and cover the sides of the cake with marzipan if wished.

Spiced Raisin Cake

Ingredients

5 oz / 10 tbsp / 150 g butter, plus extra
for greasing

2 tbsp cocoa powder, plus extra for dusting

8 eggs

½ cup / 100 g sugar

2½ cups / 250 g all-purpose
(plain) flour

1¹/₃ cups / 200 g raisins

1 tbsp cinnamon

Large pinch ground cloves

²/₃ cup / 150 ml whipping cream

1 tsp vanilla extract

Ground cinnamon

Method

Prep and cook time: 1 hour 25 min

1. Preheat the oven to 180°C (350°F / Gas Mark 4). Butter a 12 × 5 inch (30 × 12 cm) loaf pan (tin) and dust with cocoa powder.

2. Melt the butter and leave to cool slightly. Separate the eggs. Add the sugar to the egg yolks and beat together until foamy. Stir in the butter, then one after the other stir the flour, cocoa powder, raisins, cinnamon and cloves into the mixture.

3. Whisk the egg whites until stiff and carefully fold into the batter. Turn the batter into the prepared loaf pan and smooth the top.

4. Bake in the oven for about 1 hour. Leave to cool slightly in the pan, and then remove from the pan and leave to cool completely.

5. To serve, whisk the cream with vanilla extract until stiff. Spread on top of the cake and sprinkle with cinnamon.

Hazelnut and Fruit Malt Loaf

Ingredients

4 cups / 400 g strong white
bread flour

1 cup / 100 g strong wholemeal
bread flour

1 tsp salt

¼ cup / 50 g dark soft
brown sugar

2 oz / ½ stick / 50 g butter

¼ oz / 7 g easy-blend dried yeast

1¼ cups / 300 ml hand-
hot warm water

3 tbsp milk powder

3 tbsp malt extract

¾ cup / 125 g raisins

⅓ cup / 50 g hazelnuts

Method

Prep and cook time: 1 hour 20 min plus 1 hour 10 min rising time

1. Grease a 2-lb (900-g) loaf pan. Put the strong white and brown flour, salt and sugar into a large bowl. Add the butter, in small pieces, and rub the mixture together with your fingertips to incorporate the butter. Sprinkle over the dried yeast.

2. Put the warm water and milk powder into a jug. Stir in the malt extract and mix together.

3. Pour the liquid ingredients into the dry ingredients and mix together to make a rough ball.

4. Turn the dough out on to a lightly floured surface and knead for 10 minutes until smooth and elastic.

5. Put into a greased bowl, cover loosely with plastic wrap (clingfilm) and leave to rise in a warm place 30-40 minutes until doubled in size.

6. Knock back the dough on a lightly floured surface and add the raisins and hazelnuts, if using. Shape the dough into an oblong and put into the prepared loaf pan.

7. Cover loosely with clear wrap or a clean tea towel and leave to rise in a warm place for 30–40 minutes, until doubled in size.

8. Preheat the oven to 400°F (200°C / Gas Mark 6). Bake the bread in the oven for 50 minutes or until dark golden brown. The bread is cooked when the base is tapped and it sounds hollow. Leave to cool on a wire rack.

Blackberry Slices

Ingredients

Makes about 16

10 oz / 2½ sticks / 300 g butter

8 eggs

1 cup / 200 g sugar

2 tsp vanilla extract

Grated zest of ½ unwaxed lemon

1¼ cups / 125 g all-purpose (plain) flour

1½ cups / 300 g cream of wheat (semolina)

1½ tsp baking powder

3 cups / 400 g blackberries

Confectioners' (icing) sugar, for dusting

Ground pistachios, for sprinkling

Method

Prep and cook time: 1 hour

1. Preheat the oven to 350°F (180°C / Gas Mark 4). Line a baking pan (tin), measuring about 15 x 10 x ¾ inch (38 x 25 x 2 cm) with baking parchment.

2. Beat the butter until light and fluffy. Separate 6 of the eggs. Gradually beat the egg yolks and the remaining 2 whole eggs into the butter with ¾ cup / 150 g of the sugar, the vanilla extract and grated lemon zest, alternating the addition of the eggs with the other ingredients.

3. Mix the flour, cream of wheat (semolina) and baking powder together and gradually stir into the egg mixture.

4. Whisk the egg whites until stiff, gradually trickling in the remaining sugar. Carefully fold into the batter with the blackberries. Spread the batter in the prepared baking pan.

5. Bake in the oven for 35–40 minutes. Leave to cool and then dust with confectioners' (icing) sugar and sprinkle with ground pistachios. Cut into rectangles to serve.

Blackberry and Banana Tea Loaf

Ingredients

3½ oz / 7 tbsp / 100 g butter

Scant 1 cup / 175 g sugar

2 large eggs

2¼ cups / 225 g flour

2 tsp baking powder

½ tsp ground cinnamon

½ tsp ground ginger

1 large banana, peeled and mashed

1½ cups / 175 g blackberries

2 tbsp milk

2 tbsp brown sugar

Flour for dusting the pan

Method

Prep and cook time: 1 hour 15 min

1. Preheat the oven to 350°F (180°C / Gas Mark 4). Grease a 12 inch (30 cm) loaf pan and sprinkle with flour.

2. Cream the butter and sugar until light and fluffy. Then beat in the eggs one at a time, beating well between additions. Mix the flour and baking powder and sprinkle onto the mixture, then add the spices and mix in.

3. Mix in the mashed banana, blackberries and milk. Turn the batter into the prepared loaf pan, smooth the top and bake in the preheated oven for 45–50 minutes, until the cake is well risen and a wooden cocktail stick inserted into the middle comes out clean.

4. Let cool, sprinkle with brown sugar and serve in slices.

Apple and Cinnamon Muffins

Ingredients

Makes 8

4 oz / 1 stick / 125 g butter, softened

Heaped ½ cup / 125 g superfine (caster) sugar

2 large eggs

1¼ cup / 125 g all-purpose (plain) flour

1 tsp baking powder

½ tsp baking soda (bicarbonate of soda)

1 tsp cinnamon

2 large eggs

3½ oz / 100 g apple sauce

1 tsp cinnamon

For the frosting:

2 cups / 200 g confectioners' (icing) sugar

About 5 tbsp milk

1 tsp vanilla extract

½ tsp cinnamon

1 apple

Method

Prep and cook time: 40 min

1. Preheat the oven to 350°F (180°C / Gas Mark 4). Line an 8-hole muffin pan with paper muffin cases.

2. Put the butter and sugar in a large bowl and, using a hand-held electric whisk, beat together until light and fluffy.

3. Add the eggs to the mixture, one at a time, beating thoroughly after each addition.

4. Sift in the flour, baking powder, baking soda and cinnamon. Add the apple sauce and stir together until combined.

5. Divide the mixture equally between the muffin cases.

6. Bake in the oven for 25 minutes until firm or a toothpick (cocktail stick), inserted into the center, comes out clean. Leave to cool on a wire rack.

7. To make the frosting, sift the confectioners' (icing) sugar into a large bowl. Add the milk and vanilla and mix until smooth. If the icing is too stiff, add a little extra milk until a smooth dropping consistency is formed.

8. Spoon the frosting on top of the cakes. Quarter, core and chop the apple. Sprinkle the cinnamon over the cakes and top with the apple pieces.

Blueberry Muffins

Ingredients

Makes 12

2 oz / ½ stick / 50 g butter

1 egg

3 tbsp honey

Scant ½ cup / 100 ml plain yogurt

Scant ½ cup / 100 ml sour cream

2½ cups / 250 g all-purpose (plain) flour

2 tsp baking powder

2½ cups / 250 g blueberries

Confectioners' (icing) sugar, for dusting

Method

Prep and cook time: 40 min

1. Preheat the oven to 350°F (180°C / Gas Mark 4). Line a 12-hole muffin pan with paper cases. Melt the butter and leave to cool slightly, so that it is still liquid.

2. Put the egg, honey, yogurt and sour cream in a large bowl and mix together. Stir in the melted butter. Sift in the flour and baking powder and mix together. Fold in the blueberries. Fill the muffin pan three-quarters full with the batter.

3. Bake in the oven for 25-30 minutes, until golden brown. Leave to rest in the pan for 5 minutes, and then remove from the pan and leave to cool on a wire rack. Serve dusted with confectioners' (icing) sugar.

Orange Muffins with Chocolate Chips

Ingredients

Makes 12

3 cups / 300 g all-purpose (plain) flour

2½ tsp baking powder

½ tsp baking soda (bicarbonate of soda)

2 ½ oz / 75 g chopped candied orange peel

½ cup / 100 g superfine (caster) sugar

2½ oz / 70 g chocolate chips

½ cup / 100 ml vegetable oil

Generous ⅓ cup / 100 ml orange juice

Generous ¾ cup / 200 ml buttermilk

2 eggs

3 orange slices, quartered, to decorate

Method

Prep and cook time: 35 min

1. Preheat the oven to 350°F (180°C / Gas Mark 4). Line a 12-hole muffin pan with paper muffin cases.

2. Sift the flour, baking powder and baking soda into a large bowl. Add the orange peel, sugar and half the chocolate chips.

3. Pour the oil into a jug, add the orange juice, buttermilk and eggs and mix together with a fork.

4. Pour the liquid ingredients into the flour mixture and gently stir together until just combined.

5. Spoon the mixture equally into the muffin cases. Sprinkle over the remaining chocolate chips and top each muffin with an orange quarter.

6. Bake in the oven for about 25 minutes until the muffins are risen and firm. Leave to cool on a wire rack.

Cherry Muffins with Crumble Topping

Ingredients

Makes 12

3 oz / 6 tbsp / 90 g butter

3½ cups / 350 g all-purpose (plain) flour

4 tsp baking powder

1 cup / 200 g superfine (caster) sugar

Finely grated zest 1 lemon

5 oz / 150 g pitted sweet fresh or frozen cherries

2 eggs

1 cup / 250 ml milk

¾ cup / 175 g cream cheese

¼ cup / 25 g ground almonds

Method

Prep and cook time: 45 min

1. Preheat the oven to 200°C (400°F / Gas Mark 6). Line a 12-hole muffin pan with paper muffin cases.

2. Melt 5 tbsp (75 g) of the butter. Sift the flour and baking powder into a large bowl. Add a heaped ½ cup (125 g) of sugar, the lemon zest and the cherries. Stir together to coat the cherries in the flour.

3. Put the eggs and melted butter in a jug and mix together with a fork.

4. Add the liquid ingredients to the flour mixture and stir together until just combined.

5. Melt the remaining 2 tbsp of butter and set aside.

6. Put the cream cheese in a bowl and mix in 2 tbsp of the sugar.

7. Spoon half the muffin mixture equally into the muffin cases. Spoon a dollop of cream cheese into each one. Top with the remaining muffin mixture.

8. Add the remaining ¼ cup (50 g) of sugar and the ground almonds to the remaining melted butter and mix together. Sprinkle the crumble mixture over the top of each muffin.

9. Bake in the oven for 15 minutes until the muffins are well risen and firm. Leave to cool on a wire rack.

Coconut Cupcakes

Ingredients

Makes 12

6 oz / 1½ sticks / 175 g butter, softened

Heaped 1 cup / 225 g superfine (caster) sugar

2 eggs

1 tsp vanilla extract

2¼ cups / 225 g all-purpose (plain) flour

2 tsp baking powder

½ cup / 125 ml plain yogurt

6 oz / 175 g sweetened flaked coconut plus extra, to decorate

For the frosting:

1½ cups / 175 g confectioners' (icing) sugar

2 tbsp lemon juice

1 tsp hot water

Method

Prep and cook time: 45 min

1. Preheat the oven to 350°F (180°C / Gas Mark 4). Line a 12-hole muffin pan with paper muffin cases.

2. Put the butter and sugar in a large bowl and, using an electric whisk, beat together until light and fluffy. Beat in the eggs and vanilla extract.

3. Sift in the flour and baking powder and gently fold into the mixture with the yogurt, until well combined. Stir in the coconut. Spoon the mixture equally into the muffin cases.

4. Bake in the oven for 25-30 minutes until golden brown and springy to the touch. Leave in the pan for 5 minutes and then transfer to a wire rack and leave to cool.

5. When the cupcakes are cold, make the frosting. Sift the confectioners' (icing) sugar into a bowl and gradually stir in the lemon juice and water until smooth.

6. Spoon a little frosting on top of each cupcake and smooth the surface with a palette knife. Sprinkle with sweetened flaked coconut and leave to set before serving.

Gingerbread Muffins

Ingredients

Makes 12

3½ oz / 7 tbsp / 100 g butter

½ cup / 100 g soft brown sugar

3 tbsp molasses (black treacle)

½ cup / 125 ml milk

1 large egg

1½ cup / 150 g all-purpose (plain) flour

1 tbsp ground ginger

2 tbsp ground cinnamon

1 tsp baking soda (bicarbonate of soda)

Method

Prep and cook time: 40 min

1. Preheat the oven to 350°F (180°C / Gas Mark 4). Line a 12-hole muffin pan with paper muffin cases.

2. Put the butter, sugar and molasses (black treacle) in a jug. Microwave on Medium for 2 minutes or until melted together. Alternatively, heat gently together in a saucepan, and then pour into a jug.

3. Add the milk to the butter mixture and stir in the egg.

4. Sift the flour, spices and baking soda into a large bowl. Pour in the liquid ingredients and stir gently together until combined.

5. Spoon the mixture evenly between the muffin cases.

6. Bake in the oven for 20 minutes until the muffins are well risen and firm. Leave to cool on a wire rack.

Iced Cupcakes

Ingredients

Makes 12

4 oz / 1 stick / 120 g butter

½–⅔ cup / 120 g superfine (caster) sugar

2 eggs, beaten

Heaped 1 cup / 120 g self-rising flour

½ tsp baking powder

1 tsp vanilla extract

For the frosting:

1½ cups / 170 g confectioners'
(icing) sugar

2 tbsp lemon juice

1 tsp hot water

Few drops pink food coloring

Pink and white sprinkles, to decorate

Method

Prep and cook time: 35 min

1. Preheat the oven to 350°F (180°C / Gas Mark 4). Line a 12-hole muffin pan with paper cases.

2. Put the butter and sugar in a large bowl and, using an electric whisk, beat together until light and fluffy.

3. Add the eggs gradually, beating well after each addition. Sift in the flour and baking powder and gently fold into the mixture. Stir in the vanilla extract. Spoon the mixture equally into the paper cases.

4. Bake in the oven for 12–15 minutes until springy to the touch. Transfer to a wire rack and leave to cool.

5. When cold, make the frosting. Sift the confectioners' (icing) sugar into a large bowl and gradually stir in the lemon juice and water until smooth.

6. Put half the frosting in another bowl and add a few drops of pink food coloring.

7. Spoon a little frosting on each cupcake and smooth the surface with a palette knife. Decorate with pink and white sprinkles and leave to set.

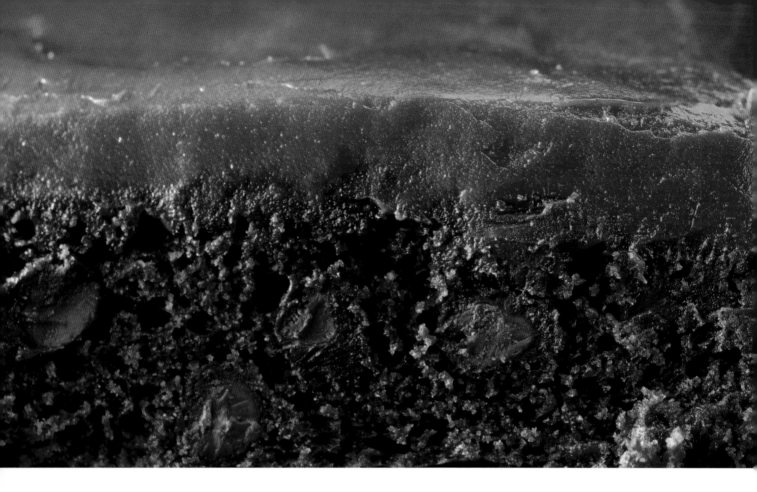

Mississippi Mud Cake

Ingredients

9 oz / 2 sticks plus 2 tbsp / 250 g butter, plus extra for greasing

Cocoa powder

1¼ cups / 300 ml strong coffee

¼ cup / 60 ml whiskey

5½ oz / 150 g dark chocolate (at least 30% cocoa solids)

Scant 2 cups / 375 g sugar

2½ cups / 250 g all-purpose (plain) flour

1 tsp baking powder

1 tsp baking soda

Pinch of salt

1 vanilla bean (pod)

2 eggs

Confectioners' (icing) sugar, for dusting

Whipped cream, to serve

Method

Prep and cook time: 2 hours

1. Preheat the oven to 250°F (120°C / Gas Mark ½). Butter a large ring cake pan (tin), measuring about 11 inches (28 cm) and dust with cocoa powder.

2. Put the coffee and whiskey in a saucepan and heat slowly. Break in the chocolate, add the butter in small pieces, and stir constantly until melted and smooth. Remove from the heat, stir in the sugar and leave to cool slightly.

3. Transfer the mixture to a large bowl and, using a hand-held electric whisk, gradually mix in the flour, baking powder, baking soda and salt at a low speed. Split and scrape out the seeds from the vanilla bean (pod) and add to the mixture. Add the eggs and mix until smooth. Pour the batter into the prepared cake pan.

4. Bake in the oven for 90–100 minutes, until a toothpick (cocktail stick) inserted into the middle comes out clean. Leave to cool slightly, and then carefully turn out on to a wire rack. Dust with confectioners' (icing) sugar and serve with whipped cream.

Chocolate Fudge Cake

Ingredients

For the cake batter:

4½ oz / 125 g bittersweet (plain) cooking chocolate (70% cocoa solids)

2 tbsp orange liqueur

4 eggs

1 pinch salt

2/3 cup / 135 g sugar

4 oz / 1 stick / 125 g soft butter

2 tbsp maple syrup

2/3 cup / 100 g whole hazelnuts, ground

½ cup / 35 g coconut flakes

4–6 chocolate caramels, chopped

Oil, to grease the frame

Flour, to coat the frame

For the fudge topping:

2 cups / 400 g sugar

½ cup / 50 g cocoa

1 cup / 240 ml milk

2 oz / ½ stick / 60 g soft butter

Vanilla extract, to taste

Method

Prep and cook time: 1 h 40 min

1. Chop the chocolate and melt with the liqueur in a bowl over a pan of hot water. Separate the eggs.

2. Beat the egg whites until stiff with a pinch of salt, gradually add a quarter of the sugar and continue beating until firm, glossy and white.

3. Cream the butter with the rest of the sugar until pale and creamy. Stir the egg yolks into the maple syrup and chocolate. Fold in the beaten egg whites, ground hazelnuts and coconut flakes. Preheat the oven to 325°F (160°C / Gas Mark 3).

4. Put a rectangular baking frame 6 x 12 inches (15 x 30 cm) on a cookie sheet lined with baking parchment. Oil the inner sides and sprinkle with flour. Fold the chopped caramels into the batter, turn the batter into the frame and bake in the oven for about 50 minutes. After 35 minutes, cover the top with kitchen foil to prevent it browning too much. Remove from the oven and let cool.

5. For the fudge topping, put the sugar, cocoa powder and milk into a pot and bring to a boil stirring constantly. Reduce the heat, do not stir any further and check the temperature with a sugar thermometer: it must be 114°C (237°F) (alternatively, drop a little of the mixture into a cup of cold water, to see if it forms smooth, malleable lumps).

6. Remove the pot from the heat and stir in the butter and the vanilla extract. Beat with a wooden spoon until the fudge is no longer shiny. Pour onto the cake, spread evenly and let cool.

Chocolate Brownies

Ingredients

For 30 brownies

5 oz / 150 g bittersweet (plain) cooking chocolate (70% cocoa solids)

7 oz / 14 tbsp / 200 g butter

6 eggs

1½ cups / 300 g dark brown sugar

2/3 cup / 150 g peanut butter

2/3 cup / 150 ml sour cream

2 cups / 200 g all-purpose (plain) flour

4 tbsp cocoa powder

5 oz / 150 g macadamia nuts, chopped

Method

Prep and cook time: 1 hour 10 min

1. Pre-heat the oven to 350°F (180°C / Gas Mark 4).

2. Break the cooking chocolate into pieces. Melt the chocolate together with the butter in a bowl over a pan of hot water. Let cool. Beat the eggs with the sugar until smooth and creamy. Add the chocolate–butter mix and the peanut butter and stir. Fold in the sour cream, followed by the flour and the cocoa. Stir in the nuts.

3. Pour onto a cookie sheet covered with parchment paper and bake on the middle shelf of the oven for 30–40 minutes. Take out of the oven and cool on a wire rack. Cut into squares.

Jelly Roll

Ingredients

5 eggs

²/₃ cup / 125 g sugar

1 tsp lemon juice

1 cup / 100 g self-rising flour

A good pinch of baking powder

2–3 tbsp cornstarch (cornflour)

Sugar for sprinkling

¼–¹/₃ cup / 100 g conserve or jelly (jam), such as raspberry or strawberry

Confectioners' (icing) sugar for dusting

Method

Prep and cook time: 30 min plus cooling time 30 min

1. Pre-heat the oven to 400°F (200°C / Gas Mark 6). Separate the eggs. Beat the egg whites until they form soft peaks, then gradually trickle in the sugar and continue beating until the mixture is firm and glossy. Add the lemon juice. Mix the flour, baking powder and cornstarch (cornflour) and gradually fold (do not stir) into the beaten egg white, alternating with additions of egg yolk.

2. Spread the batter smoothly over a cookie sheet lined with baking parchment and bake in the oven for 8–10 minutes.

3. Take out of the oven and turn out the sponge onto a tea towel sprinkled with sugar. Pull off the baking parchment and roll up the sponge. Cover with the tea towel and let cool.

4. Unroll the cooled sponge, spread with conserve or jelly and roll up again. Dust with confectioners' (icing) sugar and serve in slices.

Chocolate Ball Cake

Ingredients

7 oz / 200 g dark chocolate (64-75% cocoa solids)

4 oz / 1 stick / 125 g butter

4 eggs

⅔ cup / 125 g sugar

1½ cups / 150 g flour

1 cup / 100 g ground hazelnuts

1 tsp baking powder

In addition:

Butter for the pan

Confectioners' (icing) sugar

Method

Prep and cook time: 1 hour

1. Chop the chocolate and melt in a bowl over a pan of hot water with the butter, then set aside. Pre-heat the oven to 350°F (180°C / Gas Mark 4).

2. Beat the egg yolks and sugar until foamy and stir in the melted chocolate. Mix the flour with the ground hazelnuts and baking powder and stir into the chocolate mixture. Mix well. Beat the egg whites until stiff and fold in.

3. Grease an 11 inch /28 cm springform pan with the butter. Turn the batter into the pan and bake in the oven for about 30 minutes. Take out of the oven, cool in the pan for 10 minutes, then take out of the pan and let cool completely.

4. Draw a ball stencil on card, cut out and lay on top of the cake. Dust the cake with confectioners' sugar and carefully remove the stencil.

Gingerbread Men

Ingredients

For 10 biscuits

3 tbsp / 40 g dark brown sugar

2 tbsp golden syrup or dark corn syrup

1-inch cinnamon stick

½ tsp ground ginger

2 oz / 4 tbsp / 50 g butter, cubed

¼ tsp baking soda

1¼ cups /125 g all-purpose (plain) flour

Method

Prep and cook time: 40 min plus 30 min chilling time

1. Heat the oven to 350°F (180°C / Gas Mark 4) Lightly grease 2 baking sheets.

2. Put the sugar, syrup, cinnamon, ginger and 1 tsp of water, together in a large saucepan and heat, stirring constantly, until the sugar is dissolved. Remove from the heat, remove the cinnamon stick, and stir in the butter and baking soda.

3. Gradually stir in the flour to make a smooth manageable dough. Wrap in plastic wrap (clingfilm) and chill until firm, about 30 minutes.

4. Roll the dough out on a lightly floured surface to ⅛ inch (3mm) thickness and cut out the gingerbread men. Use the end of a small clean paint brush to press out eyes, a nose, a mouth, button and a bow tie.

5. Place cookies 2 inches (5 cm) apart on the baking sheets. Bake for 10–15 minutes or until the biscuits feel firm when lightly pressed with a fingertip.

6. Cool on the baking sheets for a few minutes before transferring them to a wire rack to cool completely.

Meringues

Ingredients

For 16–20 meringues

4 egg whites

Pinch of salt

About ¾ cup / 140–170 g sugar

2 tbsp vanilla sugar

Method

Prep and cook time: 40 min plus 4 hours drying time

1. Beat the egg whites with a pinch of salt until they form soft peaks, then gradually trickle in the sugar and vanilla sugar and continue beating until the mixture is firm and glossy. Transfer to a piping bag with a large plain nozzle.

2. Pre-heat the oven to 200°F (100°C / Gas Mark ¼). Pipe 16–20 meringues onto a cookie sheet lined with baking parchment and dry in the oven for about 4 hours, leaving the oven door open a crack. The meringues should not brown. If necessary, turn off the oven, close the door and dry for a little longer.

3. Store in an airtight container.

Brownies with Marshmallows

Ingredients

8 oz / 250 g bittersweet chocolate (min. 50% cocoa solids)

3–4 oz / 100 g mixed marshmallows

1¼ cup / 150 g confectioners' (icing) sugar

2 cups / 200 g all-purpose (plain) flour

2 tbsp cocoa

1 tsp baking powder

⅓ cup / 50 g raisins

3 eggs

⅓ cup / 80 ml maple syrup

6 oz / 1½ sticks / 180 g butter

Confectioners' (icing) sugar for dusting

Method

Prep and cook time: 50 min

1. Roughly chop 5 oz (150 g) of the chocolate, put into a small pan with the butter and stir over a low heat until melted. Pre-heat the oven to 325°F (160°C / Gas Mark 3).

2. Dice the marshmallows. Put the confectioners' (icing) sugar, flour, cocoa, baking powder and raisins into a bowl. Stir in the eggs, maple syrup and melted chocolate mixture.

3. Finely chop the rest of the chocolate and stir into the mixture with the marshmallows.

4. Grease a baking pan 9 × 12 inches (25 × 30 cm) with butter and line with baking parchment Spread the mixture in the pan and bake in the oven for 20–30 minutes. Take out, let cool slightly then take out of the tin and cool completely. Dust with confectioners' sugar and cut into squares or bars.

Chocolate Refrigerator Cake

Ingredients

1 packet butter cookies (about 4 oz /
125 g)

3½ oz / 100 g dark chocolate (60–70%
cocoa solids)

4 oz / 1 stick / 125 g butter

½ cup / 75 g confectioners' (icing) sugar

⅓ cup / 50 g raisins

Method

Prep and cook time: 30 min plus 4 hours chilling

1. Line an 8-inch (20-cm) loaf pan (tin) with plastic wrap
(clingfilm). Crush the butter cookies with a rolling pin and put a
layer of broken cookies in the bottom of the prepared loaf pan.

2. Break up the chocolate and put in a saucepan. Add the butter
and melt over a low heat, stirring. Stir in the confectioners' (icing)
sugar and raisins.

3. Stir the remaining broken cookies into the melted chocolate
mixture and turn into the loaf pan all at once. Chill in the
refrigerator for at least 4 hours.

4. To serve, turn out of the loaf pan and cut into slices using
a hot knife.

Melting Chocolate Pudding

Ingredients

For 6 ramekins

Butter to brush the ramekins, melted

4½ oz / 125 g bittersweet (plain) cooking chocolate (70% cocoa solids)

4 oz / 1 stick /125 g butter

2 eggs

3 egg yolks

⅓ cup / 65 g sugar

Pinch of salt

¼ cup / 25 g all-purpose (plain) flour

Cocoa powder, for dusting

Whipping cream, to serve

Method

Prep and cook time: 55 min plus 12 hours refrigeration

1. Brush 6 porcelain ramekins with melted butter and chill.

2. Chop the chocolate very finely and melt in a bowl over a pan of hot water with the butter. Beat the eggs, egg yolks, sugar and a pinch of salt for 8–10 minutes, until thick and creamy.

3. Then gradually fold in the melted chocolate and butter. Sieve the flour onto the mixture and fold in. Turn the mixture into the prepared ramekins and chill overnight.

4. Next day preheat the oven to 350°F (180°C / Gas Mark 4) and bake the puddings for about 15 minutes, until the middle puffs up slightly (do not open the oven while the puddings are baking).

5. The outer layer should be baked, but the center should be still liquid. Take the ramekins out of the oven and carefully turn out the pudding. Put on plates, dust with cocoa and serve with whipped cream.

Chocolate Chip Cookies

Ingredients

Makes about 20 cookies

3½ oz / 7 tbsp / 100 g soft butter

¼ cup / 50 g sugar

½ cup / 100 g brown sugar

1 large egg

1 tsp vanilla extract

1¼ cup / 130 g self-rising flour

½–⅔ cup / 100 g ground hazelnuts

1 tbsp cocoa powder

1 tsp baking powder

5 oz / 150 g bittersweet (plain) cooking chocolate (70% cocoa solids) or chocolate chips

Method

Prep and cook time: 40 min

1. Roughly chop the chocolate, if using. Preheat the oven to 350°F (180°C / Gas Mark 4). Line a cookie sheet with baking parchment.

2. Cream the butter with the sugar and brown sugar until light and fluffy. Gradually beat in the egg and the vanilla extract. Mix the flour, nuts, cocoa powder and baking powder and stir in carefully. Fold in the chopped chocolate.

3. Put teaspoonfuls of the mixture on the cookie sheet, leaving about 2 inches (5 cm) between them.

4. Bake in the oven for 10–12 minutes. Let cool on the cookie sheet for 5 minutes, then take off and cool completely on a cake rack.

Double Chocolate Chip Cookies

Ingredients

3½ oz / 7 tbsp / 100 g soft butter

¼ cup / 50 g sugar

½ cup / 100 g brown sugar

1 large egg, beaten

1 tsp vanilla extract

1¾ cups / 170 g all-purpose (plain) flour

3 tbsp cocoa powder

1 tsp baking powder

¾–1 cup / 150 g chocolate chips (70% cocoa solids)

Method

Prep and cook time: 40 min

1. Preheat the oven to 350°F (180°C / Gas Mark 4). Line a cookie sheet with baking parchment.

2. Cream the butter with the sugar and brown sugar until light and fluffy. Gradually beat in the egg and the vanilla extract. Mix the flour, cocoa powder and baking powder and carefully stir in.

3. Fold in the chocolate chips. Put teaspoonfuls of the mixture in heaps on the cookie sheet, leaving about 2 inches (5 cm) between them. Place in the oven and bake for 10–12 minutes.

4. Let cool on the cookie sheet for 5 minutes, then take off and cool on a cake rack.

Millionaire's Shortbread

Ingredients

Makes 12

12 oz / 3 sticks / 350 g butter

1⅓ cups / 250 g sugar

2¾ cups / 275 g all-purpose (plain) flour

1¼ cups / 300 ml condensed milk

¼ cup / 60 ml honey or corn syrup

For the chocolate topping:

7 oz / 200 g dark chocolate (at least 64% cocoa solids)

2 tbsp / 25 g butter

¾ oz / 15 g white chocolate

Method

Prep and cook time: 1 hour 10 min

1. Preheat the oven to 350°F (180°C / Gas Mark 4). Put 2 sticks (225 g) butter and ½ cup (100 g) sugar in a large bowl and beat together until light and fluffy. Sift in the flour and knead to a pliable dough. Press the mixture into an 11x9 inch (28x23 cm) baking pan (tin) and smooth the top.

2. Bake in the oven for 20 minutes, until set and lightly browned.

3. Meanwhile, make the caramel layer. Melt the remaining butter in a saucepan, add the remaining sugar and allow to caramelize. Add the condensed milk, stir in the honey or corn syrup, bring to a boil and simmer for about 20 minutes (or longer if necessary), stirring frequently, until the mixture is thick and caramelized. Pour over the shortbread base and leave to cool.

4. To make the chocolate topping, break the dark chocolate into a bowl. Add the butter and melt over a saucepan of simmering water. Pour over the caramel and leave to cool.

5. Melt the white chocolate in a bowl over a pan of simmering water. Put into a small paper bag, snip off one corner and drizzle over the topping to decorate. Cut into squares before serving.

Raspberry-Peach Crisp

Ingredients

Oil, for greasing

²/₃ cup / 50 g flaked almonds

2 tbsp finely chopped hazelnuts

Scant ½ cup / 100 ml honey

1 tbsp / 20 g butter

3–4 heaped tbsp fine rolled oats

4–5 peaches

2½ cups / 300 g raspberries

Juice of 1 lemon

1–2 tbsp sugar

1 tsp vanilla extract

Method

Prep and cook time: 40 min

1. Preheat the oven to 400°F (200°C / Gas Mark 6). Grease a baking sheet and line another baking sheet with baking parchment. Spread the almonds and hazelnuts out on the lined baking sheet and toast in the oven for 2–3 minutes.

2. Meanwhile, put the honey and butter into a small saucepan and bring to a boil, stirring occasionally. Boil for 5–7 minutes. Add the nuts and rolled oats to the caramelized honey, mix well and spread on the greased baking sheet. Leave to set.

3. Cut the peaches in half, remove the stones and cut the flesh into bite-size pieces. Heat the raspberries in a saucepan with the lemon juice. Stir in the sugar and vanilla extract.

4. Push half of the raspberries through a sieve to form a purée. Mix with the peaches and the remaining raspberries and divide between serving glasses.

5. Break up the set caramel and chop roughly in a food processor. Scatter over the raspberry and peach mixture and serve.

Berry Cheesecake

Ingredients

Breadcrumbs, for sprinkling

4 eggs

2½ oz / 5 tbsp / 75 g butter, plus extra for greasing

1 lb 10 oz / 750 g quark (curd) cheese

5 tbsp semolina

Scant ½ cup / 75 g sugar

1 tsp baking powder

Pinch of salt

Confectioners' (icing) sugar, for dusting

11 oz / 300 g mixed berries, such as raspberries, blueberries and redcurrants, plus extra for serving

Method

Prep and cook time: 1 hour 30 min

1. Preheat the oven to 400°F (200°C / Gas Mark 6). Grease a 10-inch (25 cm) spring-form cake pan (tin) and sprinkle breadcrumbs over the bottom. Separate the eggs. Melt the butter and leave to cool slightly.

2. Beat the butter in a large bowl until soft. Add the egg yolks and beat together. Stir in the quark, semolina, sugar, baking powder and salt and mix together until smooth.

3. Whisk the egg whites until stiff, and then carefully fold into the batter. Pour the batter into the prepared cake pan and scatter the berries over the top.

4. Bake in the oven for about 1 hour. Cover with parchment paper if the cake is getting too brown. Test with a toothpick (cocktail stick) to see if the cake is cooked. Remove from the oven and leave to cool. Before serving, dust with confectioners' (icing) sugar and serve with berries.

Raspberry-Plum Crumble

Ingredients

For the filling:

6 dark red plums, quartered, stones removed and washed

1 cup / 200 g raspberries

¼ cup / 75 g superfine (caster) sugar

For the crumble:

1 cup / 125 g all-purpose flour

3½ oz / 7 tablespoons / 100 g butter, cut into pieces

½ cup / 100 g light brown sugar

To garnish:

1 tbsp sanding (rock) sugar

Method

Prep and cook time: 45 min

1. Heat the oven to 350°F (180°C / Gas Mark 4).

2. Put the plums, raspberries and caster sugar into a saucepan with 1 tbsp water. Simmer for 5 minutes to soften the fruit.

3. Meanwhile, put the flour and butter into a food processor and whiz until the mixture forms crumbs, or put into a bowl and rub the mixture together with your fingertips. Add the brown sugar and pulse to combine.

4. Spoon the fruit into a shallow medium baking dish. Spoon the crumble mixture on top, sprinkle with sanding (rock) sugar and bake for 20 minutes or until pale golden.

Summer Pudding

Ingredients

Serves 6

2 lb 4 oz / 1 kg mixed berries, (equal quantities of redcurrants, blueberries, strawberries and raspberries)

Scant ½ cup / 80 g sugar

1⅔ cup / 400 ml redcurrant juice

¼ cup / 40 g cornstarch (cornflour)

About 1 lb 2 oz / 500 g white sliced bread

Fresh berries, to serve

Mint leaves, to decorate

Method

Prep and cook time: 20 min plus 4 hours chilling

1. Using a fork, strip the redcurrants from their stalks If large, cut the strawberries into small pieces.

2. Put half the berries in a saucepan and add the sugar and redcurrant juice. Bring to the boil then simmer for 2–3 minutes. Push the fruit through a sieve and return to the pan.

3. Mix the cornstarch (cornflour) with a little cold water, add to the fruit purée and bring to the boil, stirring all the time. Carefully stir in the rest of the fruit, quickly return to the boil and immediately remove from the heat.

4. Cut the crusts off the bread. Cut 6 circles and use to line the bases of six 6 fl oz (180 ml) molds or ramekins. Cut the remaining bread into rectangles and use to line the sides of the molds.

5. Put the prepared berries into the lined molds and put into the refrigerator to cool completely. Before serving, turn out of the molds. Serve with fresh berries and decorate with mint leaves.

Rice Pudding
with Summer Berries

Ingredients

For the baked rice pudding:

Scant ½ cup / 75 g short-grain rice

2½ cups / 600 ml milk

2 tbsp / 25 g superfine (caster) sugar

For the summer berries:

12 oz / 300 g mixed frozen summer berries, such as raspberries, redcurrants, and/or blueberries

¼ cup / 50 g superfine (caster) sugar

Method

Prep and cook time: 1 hour 15 mins

1. Heat the oven to 170°C (325°F / Gas Mark 3). Grease a 1-quart (900-ml) baking dish.

2. Add the rice, milk and sugar. Cover with foil and bake for 1 hour until the rice is tender.

3. Meanwhile, put the frozen berries into a saucepan with the sugar and 3 tbsp water. Heat for 5 minutes until the fruit is tender and the sugar is dissolved.

4. To serve, add the rice pudding to the warm summer berries.

Fruits in Red Wine

Ingredients

1 cup / 200 g dark brown sugar

1¼ cups / 300 ml water

2 cloves

1 cinnamon stick

2 star anise

1 lemon, zest and juice

1¼ cups / 300 ml red wine

3 hard pears, peeled and quartered

2 sharp apples, peeled and quartered

6 dried prunes

6 dried apricots

6 plums, halved and stoned

3 dried figs, halved

Method

Prep and cook time: 20 mins plus 45 min cooling time

1. Heat the sugar, water, spices and lemon zest and juice in a pan over a low heat, stirring until the sugar has dissolved. Bring to a boil and boil for 1 minute.

2. Add the wine and reheat.

3. Add the pears and simmer for 5-10 minutes until tender. Add the prunes, apricots, figs and plums and simmer for another 5 minutes. Add the apples and simmer for 5 minutes until all the fruits are tender.

4. Remove the spices and serve warm or cold with cream or crème fraiche.

Frozen Raspberry Yogurt

Ingredients

½ cup / 50 g sifted confectioners'
(icing) sugar

12 oz / 300 g frozen raspberries

4 tbsp honey

1 lb / 500 g low-fat plain yogurt

Fresh raspberries, to garnish

Method

Prep and cook time: 20 min plus freezing time 5 h; defrosting time 20 min

1. Put the confectioners' (icing) sugar into a food processor with the raspberries and whiz together until smooth, or mash everything together with a potato masher.

2. Add the honey and yogurt and whiz together to combine, or mix with the potato masher. Do not overprocess.

3. Spoon into a freezer-proof container, seal and freeze for several hours.

4. To serve, remove the frozen yogurt from the freezer for 20 minutes to soften slightly.

5. Garnish with fresh raspberries.

Rhubarb Ice Cream

Ingredients

9 oz / 250 g rhubarb, trimmed
and chopped

8 oz / 225 g superfine (caster) sugar

⅔ cup / 150 ml red grape juice

9 oz / 250 g full fat natural yogurt

1 lemon, juice squeezed

2 tsp vanilla extract

Method

Prep and cook time: 30 min plus 5 hours freezing time

1. Put the rhubarb, ⅓ of the sugar and the grape juice into a pan. Simmer gently for 10 minutes. Leave the mixture to cool.

2. Mix together the natural yogurt, lemon juice, vanilla extract and the rest of the sugar.

3. Take 4 popsicle (lolly) molds or espresso cups. Spoon the rhubarb mixture into the base of each one.

4. Spoon the yogurt mixture on top of the rhubarb, dividing the yogurt mix equally between each mold.

5. Carefully push a popsicle (lolly) stick half way down each one. Freeze for 5 hours.

6. Dip the base of each one in hot water to release the popsicles (lollies) from the molds.

Grilled Peaches
with Amaretti Butter and Cinnamon Ice Cream

Ingredients

1 egg yolk

1/8 cup / 30 g sugar

1 good pinch ground cinnamon

Scant 1/2 cup /100 ml light cream

3–4 oz / 80–100 g amaretti cookies

2 oz / 1/2 stick / 50 g butter, softened

6 firm ripe peaches

1 tbsp sunflower oil

Method

Prep and cook time: 30 min, plus 3 hours freezing time

1. Line a baking sheet or tray with foil or parchment.

2 In a large bowl, beat the egg yolk with the sugar for 10 minutes, until pale and creamy. Mix in the cinnamon.

3. In a separate bowl, whip the cream until stiff and fold into the mixture. Shape into 2-tablespoon portions and arrange on the prepared baking sheet; freeze until firm, about 3 hours.

4. Preheat the broiler (grill). Using 4 sheets of foil, shape small "bowls" large enough to hold three peach halves and brush each with a little oil.

5. Put the amaretti into a zip-close plastic bag; seal, squeezing out air. Crush to fine crumbs with a rolling pin. Then combine with the butter and rub together to form coarse crumbs.

6. Place three peach halves in each foil dish with the cut surface facing up; sprinkle with amaretti crumbs. Place on a baking sheet and broil (grill) until soft, about 5 minutes.

7. Put the peaches with their juices onto plates, add a portion of ice cream and drizzle with a little of the juice.

Fruit Kebabs
with Chocolate Drizzle

Ingredients

1 kiwi fruit, peeled

2 thick slices fresh pineapple, cored

2 thick slices cantaloupe, seeded

1 thick slice watermelon, seeded

2½ oz / 75 g milk chocolate, (20% cocoa solids) broken into squares

Method

Prep and cook time: 20 min

1. Cut the kiwi fruit into quarters, then halve each piece to make eighths.

2. Cut each pineapple slice into 12 chunks.

3. Cut each cantaloupe melon slice into 6 chunks.

4. Cut the watermelon slice into 12 wedges.

5. Thread alternate pieces of kiwi, pineapple, cantaloupe and watermelon slices onto 8 skewers or lolly sticks.

6. In a small microwave-safe bowl, microwave the chocolate on Medium power, stirring every 30 seconds, until just melted. Drizzle the chocolate over the fruit kebabs.

Baked Apples with Blackberries

Ingredients

4 large apples

4 tsp blackcurrant juice

2 tbsp honey

2 cinnamon sticks

Good pinch of grated lemon zest

7 oz / 200 g blackberries

Butter, to grease the dish

Method

Prep and cook time: 1 hour

1. Wash, dry and core the apples, cut in half crossways and scrape out some of the flesh with a spoon or melon baller to make small "bowls".

2. Put the blackcurrant juice into a pan with the honey, the halved cinnamon sticks and lemon zest, bring to a boil and boil until the liquid is reduced slightly. Remove from the heat and stir in the blackberries.

3. Pre-heat the oven to 350°F (180°C / Gas Mark 4). Fill the apples with the stuffing (reserving the cinnamon sticks and 2 tablespoons of blackberries to garnish) and put into a buttered, ovenproof dish.

4. Bake in the oven for about 45 minutes.

5. Put on small plates, garnish with the cinnamon sticks and the reserved blackberries and serve.

Baked Bananas
with Orange and Coconut

Ingredients

4 tsp brown sugar

4 tsp butter

2 bananas

1 orange

4 tsp shredded dried coconut

Method

Prep and cook time: 25 min

1. Heat the oven to 350°F (180°C / Gas Mark 4). Cut 4 x 8-inch (20-cm) squares of foil.

2. Put 1 tsp of sugar in the center of each foil piece, along with 1 tsp butter.

3. Slice the bananas and scatter on top of the butter and sugar mixture.

4. Use a serrated knife to cut away the orange peel and pith. Cut the orange segments away from the orange membrane, catching the juice. Scatter the orange segments over the bananas with the coconut.

5. Gather up the foil edges and pour over any reserved orange juice. Seal each parcel and place on a baking sheet. Bake for 15 minutes to warm through.

Oranges in Syrup

Ingredients

4 oranges

½ cup / 100 g brown sugar

3 tbsp orange liqueur

¾ inch / 2 cm piece of fresh ginger, sliced

Mint, to garnish

Method

Prep and cook time: 20 min plus standing time 12 hours

1. Peel the oranges, removing all the white pith and skin and cut into slices about ¼–½ inch (0.5–1 cm) thick.

2. Put the sugar into a pan with 1 cup (240 ml) water, bring to a boil and simmer for about 10 minutes. Then remove from the heat and leave to cool.

3. Add the ginger and orange liqueur and put the orange slices into the syrup. The orange slices should be covered. Cover and leave to stand overnight.

4. Take the orange slices out of the syrup and serve garnished with mint.

Jam Tarts

Ingredients
Makes 12

1¾ cups / 175 g all-purpose
(plain) flour

3 oz / 7 tbsp / 90 g butter

6 tbsp cold water

¾ cup / 250 g conserve or jelly (jam) of
your choice

Flour for working

Butter for the tartlet pan

Method
Prep and cook time: 45 min

1. Preheat the oven to 400°F (200°C / Gas Mark 6).

2. Butter and chill the tartlet pan.

3. Rub the butter into the flour until it resembles breadcrumbs, then add the water and work to a pliable dough. Roll out on a floured work surface and cut out circles a little bigger than the holes in the tartlet pan.

4. Press the pastry circles into the holes and fill each with about 1 tablespoon of conserve or jelly (jam). Cut hearts, stars or other shapes out of the pastry scraps and put one on top of each jam tart.

5. Bake the tarts in the oven for about 15 minutes. Take out of the oven, leave in the pan for a short while and then take out and cool on a cake rack.

Apple Pancakes

Ingredients

1½ cups / 150 g all-purpose
(plain) flour

½ tsp baking soda (baking powder)

3 eggs

⅔ cup / 150 ml buttermilk

2 tbsp sunflower oil

1 apple, peeled and sliced

Method
Prep and cook time: 20 min

1. Sift the flour and baking soda into a large bowl.

2. In a medium bowl, whisk together the eggs and buttermilk with 3 tbsp cold water.

3. Pour the wet ingredients into the dry and whisk everything together to make a fairly smooth batter (do not overbeat).

4. Heat the oil in a large nonstick skillet (frying pan) and add the apple. Fry gently for several minutes until softened. Turn over the apple pieces.

5. Pour in the pancake batter and cook for about 3 minutes until the underside is firm, then use a large nonstick spatula to flip the pancake. Cook for 3 more minutes, or until the pancake is cooked through.

6. Cut into wedges and serve.

Blueberry Pancakes
with Maple Syrup

Ingredients

For the pancakes:

2 eggs

2 cups / 200 g all-purpose (plain) flour

2½ tsp baking powder

Pinch of salt

1¼ cups / 300 ml milk

2 tbsp clear honey

2 cups / 200 g blueberries

Butter for frying

For the topping:

Maple syrup

Method

Prep and cook time: 20 min plus 30 min standing time

1. Separate the eggs and beat the egg whites until stiff. Put the rest of the ingredients, apart from the blueberries and butter, into a mixing bowl and beat with an electric mixer to produce a smooth batter. Let the batter rest for 30 minutes.

2. Wash and drain the blueberries and fold into the pancake batter with the beaten egg whites.

3. To make the pancakes, heat a little butter in a skillet, add a spoonful of pancake batter and spread out to a circle approximately 4–5 inches (12 cm) in diameter. Fry for 2–3 minutes on one side, then turn and cook the other side. Take out of the pan and keep warm. Continue making pancakes in this way until all the batter is used up.

4. Pile the pancakes on plates, drizzle with maple syrup and serve.

Bread Pudding with Rhubarb

Ingredients

Butter, for greasing

1 stick rhubarb

¼ cup / 50 ml white wine

4 tbsp sugar

6 slices white bread

Scant 1 cup / 200 ml whipping cream

4 eggs

Seeds from a vanilla bean (pod)

Large pinch of cinnamon

Confectioners' (icing) sugar, for dusting

Method

Prep and cook time: 45 min

1. Preheat the oven to 350°F (180°C / Gas Mark 4). Butter an ovenproof dish. Cut the rhubarb into thin strips.

2. Put the white wine in a saucepan, bring to a boil, add the rhubarb and 2 tablespoons of the sugar and simmer for about 10 minutes.

3. Arrange the bread neatly in the prepared dish, overlapping the slices. Put the cream, eggs, vanilla seeds, cinnamon and the remaining 2 tablespoons of sugar in a bowl and whisk together. Pour over the bread.

4. Place the stewed rhubarb over the top of the dish and bake in the oven for about 20 minutes, until golden brown. Dust with confectioners' (icing) sugar before serving.

Pear and Hazelnut Tart

Ingredients

2 oz / 50 g dark chocolate,
at least 70% cocoa solids

¼ cup / 50 ml espresso coffee

3 eggs

½ cup / 100 g sugar

Seeds from 1 vanilla bean (pod)

1 cup / 100 g ground hazelnuts

1 tsp baking powder

2 tbsp all-purpose (plain) flour

5–6 peeled, poached pears

2 oz /50 g dark chocolate, at least 70%
cocoa solids, to decorate

For the pastry:

2 cups / 200 g all-purpose (plain) flour

Heaped ½ cup / 60 g confectioners'
(icing) sugar

Pinch of salt

3½ oz / 7 tbsp / 100 g butter

Dried peas or beans, for baking blind

Method

Prep and cook time: 1 hour 30 min plus 1 hour chilling

1. To make the pastry, put the flour, confectioners' (icing) sugar and salt in a bowl. Chop the butter into small pieces, add to the flour and using a knife or your fingertips, rub in until the mixture resembles coarse breadcrumbs. Combine all ingredients and knead to form a soft dough. Wrap in plastic wrap (clingfilm) and chill in the refrigerator for 1 hour.

2. Preheat the oven to 180°C (350°F / Gas Mark 4). Roll out the pastry on a lightly floured surface and use to line a 10 inch (25 cm) tart pan (tin), allowing 2 inch (5 cm) to hang over the edge. Place a sheet of parchment paper on the pastry and put the dried beans on top. Bake in the oven for about 15 minutes, until set. Remove the baking parchment and dried beans and leave to cool.

3. To make the filling, melt the chocolate in the espresso. Beat the eggs and sugar together until light and creamy. Stir in the vanilla seeds and the espresso chocolate. Mix the ground hazelnuts, baking powder and flour together in a bowl, and then fold into the eggs.

4. Drain and cut the pears in half, and arrange them in the pastry case. Pour the filling on top and smooth. Bake in the oven for about 40 minutes. Test with a toothpick (cocktail stick) to see if the cake is cooked. If the cake is becoming too brown, cover with a piece of foil. Remove from the oven, leave to cool, and then carefully remove the tart from the pan.

5. To decorate, melt the chocolate in a bowl, standing over a saucepan of simmering water, and then drizzle thin lines over the top of the tart in a criss-cross pattern.

Crème Caramel
with Berries

Ingredients

Scant 1 cup / 175 g sugar

Scant ½ cup / 100 ml milk

2 eggs

2 egg yolks

1 cup / 250 ml whipping cream

2 cups / 200 g mixed berries, of your choice

Method

Prep and cook time: 40 min plus 3 hours chilling

1. Preheat the oven to 325°F (170°C / Gas Mark 3). Put a deep baking pan (tin), three-quarters filled with boiling water, in the oven.

2. Put ⅓ cup (70 g) sugar in a heavy-based saucepan and heat until lightly caramelized. Put 1 tablespoon of the caramel into 4 shallow ovenproof dishes, measuring 4–5 inch (10–13 cm) in diameter.

3. Warm the milk in a pan. Put the eggs, egg yolks, remaining sugar, cream and warm milk in a bowl and whisk together. Strain through a sieve and pour on to the caramel in the dishes.

4. Place the 4 filled dishes in the pan containing the hot water and cook in the oven for about 30 minutes. Test to see if they are cooked by inserting a toothpick (cocktail stick) in the center. Leave to cool, and then chill in the refrigerator for at least 3 hours.

5. To serve, briefly dip the dishes in hot water, run the tip of a knife around the rim and turn out on to dessert plates. Serve with fresh berries of your choice.

Profiteroles
with Peaches and Cream

Ingredients

½ cup / 100 g canned sliced peaches

⅔ cup / 150 ml whipping cream

1 tbsp vanilla sugar

Confectioners' (icing) sugar, for dusting

For the choux pastry:

3½ oz / 7 tbsp / 100 g butter, plus extra
for greasing

1½ cups / 150 g all-purpose (plain) flour,
plus extra for dusting

1 tbsp cornstarch (cornflour)

1 cup / 250 ml water

½ tsp salt

4 eggs

Method
Prep and cook time: 1 hour

1. Preheat the oven to 350°F (180°C / Gas Mark 4). Grease a baking sheet and lightly dust with flour. To make the choux pastry, mix the flour and cornstarch (cornflour) together. Bring the water to a boil in a large saucepan and add the salt. Add the butter and let it melt. Tip the flour mixture into the water all at once, stirring constantly until the mixture forms a smooth ball. Beat the pastry mixture over the heat for a further 2 minutes.

2. Transfer the mixture to a mixing bowl and gradually beat in the eggs, one at a time, only adding the next egg when the previous one is completely mixed in.

3. Spoon the pastry mixture into a piping bag fitted with a large plain nozzle and pipe 4–6 balls on to the prepared baking sheet.

4. Bake in the oven for 20–25 minutes. Split the profiteroles immediately to release the steam, but don't take them apart. Leave to cool completely.

5. To fill the profiteroles, drain the peaches. Whisk the cream until stiff. Fill the profiteroles with peach slices sprinkled with sugar and sweetened whipped cream. Put the lids on, dust with confectioners' (icing) sugar and serve.

Panna Cotta with Berries

Ingredients

1 vanilla bean

2 cups / 500 ml whipping cream

¼ cup / 50 g sugar

3 leaves white gelatin (gelatine)

½ tsp lemon zest

½ lb / 225 g raspberries, to garnish

Method

Prep and cook time: 15 min plus chilling time at least 5 hours

1. Slice the vanilla bean in half lengthwise. Scrape out the seeds.

2. Cook the cream with the sugar, vanilla seeds and pod over low heat for about 3 minutes.

3. Soften the gelatin (gelatine) in a dish with cold water.

4. Remove the vanilla bean from the cream. Remove the pan from the heat.

5. Squeeze out the gelatin and add it to the vanilla cream. Stir to dissolve. Add the lemon zest.

6. Rinse out 4 molds with cold water. Fill with the cream and refrigerate for at least 5 hours.

7. Turn the panna cotta out of the molds (to dislodge: dip the molds in hot water). Garnish with the raspberries and serve.

Tiramisu

Ingredients

5 egg yolks

½ cup / 50 g confectioners' (icing) sugar

2 cups / 500 g mascarpone

3 tbsp almond liqueur

2 cups / 500 ml strong espresso

16 lady fingers (sponge fingers)

Cocoa powder, for dusting

Confectioners' (icing) sugar, for dusting

Method

Prep and cook time: 30 min

1. Beat the egg yolks and confectioners' (icing) sugar until foaming, then stir in the mascarpone and the liqueur.

2. Put the espresso in a flat dish, dip half of the lady (sponge) fingers in the espresso and lay them on the base of a rectangular serving dish.

3. Spread with half of the egg/cream mixture and dust with cocoa. Repeat the process with the remaining sponge fingers and mascarpone cream. Dust with cocoa and confectioners' sugar before serving.

Chocolate Fondue
with Fruit

Ingredients

1lb 12 oz / 800 g mixed fresh fruit, such as pear, nectarine, gooseberry, banana and fig

¾–1 cup / 200 ml whipping cream

8 oz / 250 g bittersweet (plain) cooking chocolate (70% cocoa solids)

½ tsp orange zest, finely grated

4 tbsp orange juice

4 tsp orange liqueur, according to taste

4 tbsp coconut flakes

4 tbsp nuts, chopped

Method
Prep and cook time: 30 min

1. Wash and trim the fruit, peel if necessary, and cut into bite-size pieces.

2. Arrange the fruit decoratively on a plate.

3. Put the cream and the broken chocolate pieces into a saucepan and melt the chocolate over a low heat, stirring continually. Stir in the orange zest and the orange juice.

4. Transfer the chocolate to a fondue pot and place over a burner. Add a little orange liqueur to taste.

5. Slide pieces of fruit onto a fondue fork or wooden toothpick and dip into the sauce. Serve with chopped nuts and coconut flakes.

Coffee Mousse

Ingredients

5 oz / 150 g milk chocolate, at least 30% cocoa solids

2 leaves gelatin (gelatine)

4 tbsp instant coffee powder

1½ cups / 300 ml whipping cream

2 eggs

1½ tbsp coffee liqueur

Pinch of salt

2½ tbsp sugar

Whipped cream, to serve

Cocoa powder, to decorate

Method
Prep and cook time: 40 min plus 4 hours chilling

1. Break up the chocolate and melt in bowl standing over a pan of simmering water. Soak the gelatin (gelatine) in cold water. Mix the coffee powder with a scant ½ cup (100 ml) of the cream.

2. Separate 1 egg and beat the egg yolk and the whole egg with the coffee cream in a bowl standing over a pan of simmering water, until thick and creamy. Squeeze out the gelatin and stir into the mixture until dissolved. Remove the bowl from the heat and add the chocolate and coffee liqueur. Stir until cold.

3. Whisk the egg white with a pinch of salt until stiff, trickling in the sugar at the same time. Whisk the remaining cream until stiff and fold both into the coffee mixture.

4. Divide the mousse between 4 dishes and chill in the refrigerator for at least 4 hours.

5. To serve, add a topping of whipped cream and dust with cocoa powder to decorate.

Buttermilk Biscuits

Ingredients

Makes 8

2½ cups / 250 g all-purpose (plain) flour

1 tbsp baking powder

1 tsp baking soda (bicarbonate of soda)

Pinch of salt

2 oz / ½ stick / 50 g butter

2 tbsp superfine (caster) sugar

1 cup / 250 ml buttermilk

1 tsp vanilla extract

1 tbsp milk, to glaze

Method

Prep and cook time: 30 min

1. Preheat the oven to 425°F (220°C / Gas Mark 7). Place an ungreased baking sheet into the oven, to heat up.

2. Put the flour, baking powder, salt and butter, cut into small pieces, into a food processor or large bowl. Whiz the mixture for a few seconds to form crumbs, or rub together with your fingertips.

3. Add the sugar, buttermilk and vanilla extract and just blend to combine, or use a knife to mix everything together.

4. Knead the dough lightly on a floured surface until it becomes smooth.

5. Roll out the dough to a thickness of about 1 inch (2.5 cm).

6. Dip a 2½-inch (6-cm) plain round cutter in some flour and then use it to stamp out 8 rounds of dough.

7. Use a palette knife to lift the biscuits on to the preheated baking sheet and brush the tops with milk.

8. Bake in the oven for 12–15 minutes until the biscuits are risen and pale golden brown. Serve warm or transfer to a wire rack to cool.

Apple Scones

Ingredients

Makes 8

2¼ cups / 225 g all-purpose (plain) flour

2 tsp baking powder

1 tsp baking soda (bicarbonate of soda)

Pinch of salt

3 tbsp superfine (caster) sugar

2 oz / ½ stick / 50 g butter

1 apple

1 egg

⅓ cup / 75 ml milk, plus extra to glaze

Method

Prep and cook time: 30 min

1. Preheat the oven to 230°C (450°F / Gas Mark 8). Place an ungreased baking sheet in the oven to heat.

2. Sift the flour, baking powder, baking soda, salt and add 2 tbsp of the sugar into a large bowl.

3. Cut the butter into cubes, add to the flour mixture and rub in with your fingertips until the mixture forms crumbs.

4. Peel, core and finely chop the apple. Add to the dry ingredients and stir to coat in the flour mixture.

5. Put the egg and milk in a jug and mix together with a fork. Gradually pour into the flour mixture and bring the mixture together with your hands to make a soft, manageable dough.

6. Roll out the dough on a lightly floured surface to ¾ inch (2 cm) thickness. Using a 2-inch (5-cm) plain round cutter, cut out 8 rounds.

7. Use a palette knife to lift the scones on to the preheated baking sheet. Brush with milk and sprinkle with the remaining sugar.

8. Bake in the oven for 8–10 minutes until well risen, firm and pale golden. Leave to cool on a wire rack.

Farmhouse White Loaf

Ingredients

5 cups / 500 g strong white bread flour

1 tbsp superfine (caster) sugar

1½ tsp salt

1 tsp easy-blend dried yeast

2 tbsp milk powder

1 oz / 2 tbsp / 25 g butter

1½ cups / 350 ml tepid water

Method

Prep and cook time: 30 min plus 1 hour rising time

1. Grease a 2-lb (900-g) loaf pan (tin). Put the flour, sugar and salt into a large bowl. Sprinkle over the dried yeast and milk powder.

2. Add the butter, in small pieces, and pour in the warm water. Bring the mixture together with your hands to make a rough ball.

3. Turn the dough out on to a lightly floured surface and knead for 10 minutes until smooth and elastic.

4. Cover loosely with plastic wrap (clingfilm) or a clean tea towel and leave to rise in a warm place for about 30 minutes until doubled in size.

5. Knock back the dough on a lightly floured surface and knead for a few minutes. Shape into a rectangle. Put the dough into the prepared loaf pan.

6. Cover with a clean tea towel and leave for a further 30 minutes until the dough has risen to the top of the pan.

7. Preheat the oven to 400°F (200°C / Gas Mark 6). Bake the bread in the oven for 35 minutes until golden brown. The bread is cooked when the base is tapped and it sounds hollow. Leave to cool on a wire rack.

Soda Bread

Ingredients

Makes 1 loaf

3½ cups / 350 g wholemeal flour

2 tsp baking soda (bicarbonate of soda)

1 tsp salt

1 cup / 125 g coarse oatmeal

1 tsp runny honey

1⅓ cups / 300 ml buttermilk

About 3 tbsp milk

Method

Prep and cook time: 50 min

1. Preheat the oven to 400°F (200°C / Gas Mark 6). Grease a baking sheet. Sift the flour, baking soda and salt into a large bowl. Stir in the oatmeal.

2. Add the honey, buttermilk and enough milk to form a soft dough.

3. Turn the dough out on to a lightly floured surface and knead for 5 minutes until smooth and elastic.

4. Shape the dough into a 8-inch (20-cm) round and put on the prepared baking sheet. Cut a deep cross into the center of the dough and brush with a little milk.

5. Bake in the oven for 30–35 minutes until the bread is risen and firm to the touch. The bread is cooked when the base is tapped and it sounds hollow. Leave to cool on a wire rack.

Cheese and Potato Muffins

Ingredients

Makes 12

4–5 oz / 125 g potato

2½ oz / 5 tbsp / 75 g butter

1½ cups / 150 g all-purpose (plain) flour

¾ cup / 100 g cornstarch (cornflour)

1 tbsp baking powder

½ tsp salt

1 tbsp sugar

1 tsp fresh thyme leaves

1 cup / 225 ml milk

1 egg

1½ oz / 40 g Swiss (Gruyère) cheese, plus extra to serve

Tomato salsa, to serve

Method

Prep and cook time: 40 min

1. Cut the potato into small cubes, put in a saucepan, cover with salted water and bring to the boil. Simmer for 10 minutes until almost tender.

2. Preheat the oven to 400°F (200°C / Gas Mark 6). Grease a 12-hole muffin pan or line with paper muffin cases.

3. Sift the flour and cornstarch (cornflour), baking powder and salt into a large bowl. Add the sugar and thyme.

4. Put the milk and egg into a jug. Grate in the cheese and whisk together with a fork. Melt two thirds of the butter.

5. Drain the potatoes and add to the flour mixture. Pour the liquid ingredients into the dry ingredients and stir together until just combined. Spoon the mixture equally into the greased pan or muffin cases.

6. Bake in the oven for 15–20 minutes until the muffins are firm to the touch and a toothpick (cocktail stick) inserted into the center, comes out clean. Leave to cool in the pan for 3 minutes and then transfer to a wire rack and leave to cool.

7. Dice the remaining butter and serve the muffins topped with a knob of butter, garnished with watercress and some tomato salsa. Good served with extra cheese.

Mozzarella, Tomato and Polenta Muffins

Ingredients

Makes 9

18 cherry tomatoes

2½ cups / 250 g plain (white) flour

Heaped ⅓ cup / 50 g polenta

1 tbsp superfine (caster) sugar

1 tbsp baking powder

Salt and pepper

1 tbsp torn fresh basil leaves, plus some sprigs to garnish

12 sun blushed tomatoes

2½ oz / 75 g mozzarella cheese

1 cup / 250 ml milk

2 large eggs, lightly beaten

4 tbsp olive oil

4 tsp grated Parmesan cheese

Method

Prep and cook time: 40 min

1. Preheat the oven to 375°F (190°C / Gas Mark 5). Line a 9-hole muffin pan with paper muffin cases.

2. Cut the tomatoes in half and put into a greased roasting pan (tin).

3. Sift the flour and baking powder into a large bowl. Add the polenta, sugar and torn basil leaves and season generously with salt and pepper.

4. Chop the sun blushed tomatoes and the mozzarella cheese and add to the dry ingredients.

5. Put the milk, eggs and olive oil into a jug and whisk together with a fork. Pour the liquid ingredients into the flour mixture and gently stir together with a large spoon until moistened. The batter should still be lumpy.

6. Spoon the mixture equally into the paper muffin cases. Sprinkle over the Parmesan cheese.

7. Bake the tomatoes and muffins in the oven for 20 minutes until the muffins are well risen and firm to the touch, and the tomatoes are tender.

8. Serve the muffins topped with the roasted tomatoes and garnish with basil sprigs.

Rosemary Bread

Ingredients

2 eggs

1 tsp easy-blend dried yeast

4 cups / 400 g strong white bread flour

3 tbsp chopped fresh rosemary

1 tbsp superfine (caster) sugar

4 tbsp extra virgin olive oil

Method

Prep and cook time: 1 hour 10 min plus 40 min rising time

1. Grease a 2-lb (900-g) loaf pan (tin). Put the eggs into a measuring jug and whisk together with a fork. Add warm water, to make up to the volume of 9 fl oz (275 ml).

2. Pour the liquid into a bowl, sprinkle over the yeast and add the flour, rosemary, sugar and olive oil. Bring the mixture together with your hands.

3. Turn the dough out on to a lightly floured surface and knead for 10 minutes until smooth and elastic.

4. Shape the dough into an oblong and put into the prepared loaf pan.

5. Cover loosely with plastic wrap (clingfilm) or a clean tea towel and leave to rise in a warm place for about 40 minutes until doubled in size.

6. Preheat the oven to 400°F (200°C / Gas Mark 6). Bake the bread in the oven for 45–50 minutes until golden brown. The bread is cooked when the base is tapped and it sounds hollow. Leave to cool on a wire rack.

Focaccia
with Olives and Tomatoes

Ingredients

4 ½ cups / 425 g strong white bread flour

Sea salt

1/3 cup / 40 g grated Parmesan cheese

1/3 cup / 50 g sun dried tomatoes, drained

2 tbsp sun dried tomato paste

1/3 cup / 50 g pitted black olives

3 tbsp olive oil

1 tbsp fresh thyme leaves

1 tbsp chopped fresh oregano leaves

¼ oz / 7 g easy-blend dried yeast

1 1/3 cups / 325 ml hand-hot warm water

Fresh oregano and thyme, to garnish

Method

Prep and cook time: 1 hour plus 40 min rising time

1. Grease a baking sheet. Put the flour, 1 tsp salt, Parmesan cheese, sun-dried tomatoes, sun-dried tomato paste, olives, oil, thyme and oregano into a large bowl.

2. Sprinkle over the dried yeast and then pour in the warm water. Mix together with your hands until mixture combines to make a rough dough ball.

3. Turn the dough out on to a lightly floured surface and knead for 10 minutes until smooth and elastic.

4. Shape the dough into an oval measuring about 8 x 12 in (20 x 30 cm). Put on the prepared baking sheet and press lots of indentations into the top of the bread with your finger.

5. Drizzle over the olive oil and some sea salt. Cover loosely with plastic wrap (clingfilm) or a clean tea towel and leave to rise in a warm place for 30–40 minutes until doubled in size.

6. Preheat the oven to 400°F (200°C / Gas Mark 6). Bake the bread in the oven for about 35 minutes until golden brown. The bread is cooked when the base is tapped and it sounds hollow. Leave to cool on a wire rack. Serve garnished with fresh oregano and thyme.

DRINKS AND SMOOTHIES

Pear and Orange Crush

Ingredients

Serves 2

4 pears, peeled, cored and quartered

2½ cups / 600 ml water

Juice of 4 oranges

1 tbsp honey

Method

Prep and cook time: 15 min plus 1 hour cooling

1. Put the pears into a pan and cover with the water. Bring to a boil; reduce the heat and simmer for 5 minutes to soften the fruit.

2. Turn off the heat and let stand for 10 minutes.

3. Pour the pears and juice into a blender and pulse until completely smooth.

4. Pour the pear juice through a sieve into a pitcher. Add the orange juice and honey and transfer to a bottle. Refrigerate for 1 hour. Shake before serving.

Carrot, Mango and Orange Juice

Ingredients

Serves 2

2 large carrots, peeled

1¼ cups / 300 ml cold water

1 mango, flesh cut from stone

²/₃ cups / 150 ml orange juice

To garnish:

1 celery stick, cut into slices

A few walnuts

Method

Prep and cook time: 30 min

1. Grate the carrots and put into a bowl with the cold water. Cover and leave for 20 minutes.

2. Score the mango flesh and remove from the skin, then put into a blender with the orange juice. Whiz together to combine.

3. Hold a sieve over the blender and strain the carrot juice into it, discarding the carrots. Whiz again to combine.

4. Pour into 2 glasses, add some celery and a couple of walnuts as garnish.

Orange and Peach Drink

Ingredients

Serves 2

4 peaches, quartered

4 oranges, peeled, quartered

2 sprigs fresh mint, to garnish

Method

Prep and cook time: 15 min plus 1 hour cooling

1. Remove the stones from the peaches.

2. Press the peaches and oranges through a juicer.

3. Garnish each glass with mint leaves.

Raspberry and Peach Drink

Ingredients

Serves 2

1 peach, coarsely chopped

½ cup / 100 g raspberries

2 tbsp honey

1 tbsp flaked (slivered) almonds

2 tsp lemon juice

¼ cup / 50 ml grape juice

6 ice cubes

Well chilled sparkling mineral water, as needed

Method

Prep and cook time: 15 min

1. Place the peach, raspberries, honey, almonds, lemon juice, grape juice and ice cubes in a blender and pulse to a smooth purée.

2. Divide between two glasses; add mineral water to fill.

Cappuccino Smoothie

Ingredients

Serves 2

1 1/3 cups / 300 ml strong espresso coffee

2 handfuls crushed ice

1 1/3 cups / 300 ml milk

2 tbsp maple syrup

2 tsp dark chocolate, finely grated

Method

Prep and cook time: 5 min plus 30 min cooling time

1. Pour the espresso coffee into a jug and cool.

2. Put a couple of handfuls of crushed ice into a blender and add the coffee, milk and maple syrup.

3. Whiz everything together until smooth.

4. Pour into 2 glasses and sprinkle over the finely grated chocolate to serve.

Vanilla Smoothie Brulée

Ingredients

Serves 2

½ cup / 75 g cubed honeydew melon

1 firm banana, cut into chunks

1 cup / 250 g plain yogurt

1 vanilla bean, slit lengthwise and seeds scraped out

8 ice cubes

¹/₃–½ cup / 100 ml heavy whipping cream

1 tbsp lime juice, or to taste

2 tsp brown sugar

Method

Prep and cook time: 15 min

1. Place the melon, banana, yogurt and vanilla seeds into a blender and pulse until smooth.

2. Continue blending, gradually adding the cream and ice cubes, until very creamy. Add lime juice to taste.

3. Divide the smoothie between two glasses and sprinkle with brown sugar.

4. Using a cook's blowtorch, caramelize the sugar on the surface of the smoothies and serve at once.

Coconut and Banana Shake

Ingredients

Serves 2

1 ripe banana, peeled and chopped

¹/₃–½ cup / 100 ml orange juice

¹/₃–½ cup / 100 ml coconut milk, chilled

¹/₃–½ cup / 100 ml buttermilk, chilled

1 tbsp brown sugar

Coconut flakes, to garnish

Method

Prep and cook time: 10 min

1. Put the banana, orange juice, coconut milk, buttermilk and brown sugar into a blender and pulse until smooth.

2. Pour into 2 glasses and serve garnished with coconut flakes.

Pear Yogurt Shake with Cinnamon

Ingredients

Serves 2

1 medium-sized, ripe pear, peeled, quartered, cored and chopped

Scant cup / 200 ml plain yogurt

²/₃ cup / 150 ml heavy whipping cream

1 tbsp acacia honey

½ tsp ground cinnamon

1 pinch nutmeg

Cinnamon sugar, to garnish

Method

Prep and cook time: 15 min

1. Put the pear, yogurt, cream, honey, cinnamon and nutmeg in a blender and pulse until smooth. For best results, the pear should be soft but not mushy. Yogurt and cream should be well chilled.

2. Pour into glasses and sprinkle with cinnamon sugar to serve.

Blueberry Smoothie

Ingredients

Serves 2

$^1/_3$ cup / 50 g blueberries

$^1/_3$ cup / 50 g redcurrants

2 tbsp brown sugar

3 tbsp desiccated coconut, toasted in a dry pan and cooled

$^1/_3$–$^1/_2$ cup / 100 ml coconut milk

Generous ¾ cup / 200 ml milk

Method

Prep and cook time: 15 min plus 30 mins chilling

1. Lay the blueberries and redcurrants in a shallow dish and place in the freezer for about 30 minutes.

2. Purée the berries, sugar, 2 tbsp of the desiccated coconut, coconut milk and milk in a blender.

3. Pour into two glasses and serve sprinkled with the remaining desiccated coconut.

Blackberry and Apple Smoothie

Ingredients

Serves 2

1¼ cups / 250 g frozen blackberries

2 tbsp honey

1 cup / 250 g forest fruits or blueberry yogurt

1$^1/_3$ cups / 300 ml pressed apple juice

4 frozen blackberries, to garnish

Method

Prep and cook time: 5 min

1. Put the frozen blackberries into a blender with the honey, yogurt and apple juice. Pulse until smooth and pour into 2 glasses.

2. Thread blackberries onto 2 bamboo skewers or cocktail sticks and garnish the smoothies.

Tomato Gazpacho Smoothie

Ingredients

Serves 2

14 oz / 400 g can tomatoes

Half red bell pepper, seeds removed

Half cucumber, chopped

1 tbsp balsamic vinegar

1 tbsp cillantro (coriander)

1 scallion (spring onion), chopped

1 garlic clove, peeled

Dash chili sauce

Couple of handfuls crushed ice

Method

Prep and cook time: 10 min

1. Open the can of tomatoes and tip into a blender.

2. Roughly chop the red bell pepper and add to the blender with the cucumber.

3. Add the balsamic vinegar, cilantro (coriander), scallion (spring onion), garlic and chili sauce.

4. Whiz everything together with a couple of handfuls of crushed ice.

5. Pour into 2 glasses and garnish each one with a sprig of watercress.

Acai Berry and Raspberry Smoothie

Ingredients

Serves 2

1¼ cups / 300 ml acai berry juice

12 oz / 350 g frozen raspberries

1 cup / 250 g natural yogurt

2 tbsp runny honey

To garnish:

Some raspberries

1 tsp demerara sugar

Method

Prep and cook time: 5 min

1. Put the acai berry juice into a blender. Add the raspberries, yogurt and honey.

2. Whiz together until blended and really smooth. Pour into 2 glasses.

3. Dip the ends of 6 raspberries into the smoothie, then dip these raspberry tips into the demerara sugar. Thread 3 onto 2 wooden skewers or cocktail sticks to serve.

Kiwi Fruit, Melon and Pear Smoothie

Ingredients

Serves 2

2 kiwi fruit, peeled and chopped

¾ cup / 150 g chopped honeydew melon

1 small, very ripe pear, peeled, cored and chopped

2 tbsp lemon juice

6 ice cubes

Confectioners' (icing) sugar to taste

Method

Prep and cook time: 15 min

1. Place the kiwi fruit, melon and pear into a blender with the lemon juice and ice; pulse until smooth.

2. Add confectioners' (icing) sugar to taste and serve.

Mango and Pineapple Smoothie

Ingredients
Serves 2

2 large, ripe mangos, peeled

Juice of 1 lime, zest peeled off in thin strips and reserved

A few ice cubes

^{1}/3–½ cup / 100 ml pineapple juice

1–2 tbsp honey

Well-chilled still mineral water, if required

Garnish:

Fresh mint leaves

Reserved lime zest

Method
Prep and cook time: 10 min plus 30 min chilling time

1. Cut the flesh away from either side of the mango stone and chop the flesh.

2. Lay the chopped mango in a shallow dish and place in the freezer for about 30 minutes.

3. Blend the mango, lime juice, ice cubes, pineapple juice and honey in a blender. Well-chilled water can be added if necessary.

4. Divide the smoothie between two glasses and garnish with the strips of lime zest and mint leaves.

Mango and Banana Smoothie

Ingredients
Serves 2

1 mango, flesh cut away from stone

2 bananas, sliced

1 cup / 250 g natural yogurt

6 tbsp crushed ice

1 passion fruit, halved, to garnish

Method
Prep and cook time: 15 min

1. Score the mango flesh into slices and cut away from the skin. Reserve a couple of slices of mango.

2. Put the rest of the mango into a blender with the banana and natural yogurt. Whiz together until smooth.

3. Add the crushed ice and blend together again. Pour into 2 glasses.

4. Scoop out the seeds and juice from the passion fruit and spoon on top of the smoothies with the reserved mango slices.

Peach and Passion Fruit Smoothie

Ingredients
Serves 2

1 1-lb / 450-g can peaches in natural juice

1 banana, sliced

^{2}/3 cup / 150 ml passion fruit juice

^{2}/3 cup / 150 ml lowfat milk

1 passion fruit, halved, to garnish

Method
Prep and cook time: 5 min

1. In a blender or food processor, combine the canned peaches and their juice, banana, passion fruit juice and milk. Pulse until completely smooth and pour into 2 glasses.

2. Scoop out the passion fruit seeds and spoon them on top of each smoothie to garnish.

Frozen Strawberry Drink

Ingredients

Serves 2

1 pint / 250 g strawberries

1/3 cup / 100 ml apple juice

2 tsp superfine (caster) sugar

2 tbsp lime juice

8 tbsp crushed ice

Garnish:

Fresh lemon balm leaves

Reserved strawberry

Method

Prep and cook time: 40 min plus 30 min chilling time

1. Lay the strawberries out in a single layer on a tray and place in the freezer for 30 minutes to freeze slightly. Reserve a strawberry for the garnish.

2. Place the strawberries, apple juice, sugar, lime juice and ice in a blender and pulse to a coarse purée.

3. Pour into glasses to serve and garnish with lemon balm and the reserved strawberry.

Iced Melon Juice

Ingredients

Serves 2

½ small honeydew melon, seeded and cut into chunks

1 tsp maple syrup

2 tbsp lime juice

8 ice cubes

1 cup / 250 ml sparkling mineral water

Garnish:

Melon balls, threaded onto wooden skewers

Fresh mint leaves

Method

Prep and cook time: 15 min

1. Place the melon, maple syrup, lime juice and 4 ice cubes in a blender and blend thoroughly.

2. Divide between two glasses and add the remaining ice cubes. Add mineral water to fill.

3. Garnish with the melon ball skewers and mint leaves.

Lemon Grass Lemonade

Ingredients

Serves 2

1 stem lemon grass

Zest and juice of 2 large lemons

¼ cup / 50 g superfine (caster) sugar

2½ cups / 600 ml boiling water

10 ice cubes

Garnish:

2 stems lemon grass

2 mint sprigs

Method

Prep and cook time: 15 min plus 8 hours chilling

1. Trim off the base and top of the lemon grass stem, finely slice the remainder. Put the sliced lemon grass into a heatproof bottle or container and add the lemon juice, zest and sugar.

2. Pour over the boiling water. Cover and let steep overnight.

3. Stir and taste for sweetness, adding more sugar if needed. Strain the lemonade into 2 glasses.

4. Add ice cubes to fill and garnish with a lemon grass stem and mint sprig in each glass.

Chilled Fruit Cocktail

Ingredients

Serves 2

1 cup / 200 g mixed fruit (try grapefruit, apple, black grapes) cut into bite-size pieces

1 cup / 200 ml apple juice

2 tbsp lime juice

6 ice cubes

About 1 cup / 200 ml well-chilled sparkling mineral water

Method

Prep and cook time: 15 min

1. Thread the prepared fruit onto wooden skewers.

2. Pour the apple juice and lime juice into a blender. Add the ice cubes and pulse briefly.

3. Divide the juice between two glasses and add the fruit skewers. Add mineral water to fill.

Hot Honey and Lemon with Cloves

Ingredients

3 lemons, halved

1¼ cups / 300 ml water

4 tsp honey

1 tsp whole cloves (optional)

Method

Prep and cook time: 5 min

1. Squeeze the juice from 5 of the lemon halves and pour into a heatproof pitcher with 1¼ cups / 300 ml boiling water, stirring well.

2. Put 2 tsp honey into each of 2 warmed glasses and add hot lemonade to fill.

3. Cut the remaining lemon half into wedges, stud with cloves (note – they have a strong flavor!) and place in the glasses.

Warm Apple Punch

Ingredients

Serves 2

2 cups / 500 ml apple juice

1 cinnamon stick

4 juniper berries

Zest and juice of 1 orange

Red apple peel, for garnishing

2 cinnamon sticks, for garnishing

Method

Prep and cook time: 30 min

1. Put the apple juice, cinnamon stick and juniper berries into a large saucepan.

2. Add the orange zest and juice to the saucepan; bring to a boil, reduce the heat and simmer for 20 minutes to infuse the spices.

3. Strain the punch and ladle into 2 heatproof glasses. Garnish each with a cinnamon stick and a swirl of apple peel.

Chili Mango Cocktail

Ingredients

Serves 2

4 thin slices red chilli

2 tbsp lime juice

4 tsp agave syrup

1/3–½ cup/ 100 ml elderflower cordial

2/3 cup / 150 ml mango juice

A couple of handfuls of ice cubes

4 tbs grenadine

Method

Prep and cook time: 10 min

1. Put the chili slices into a cocktail shaker and mash (muddle) with a long spoon.

2. Add the lime juice, agave syrup, elderflower cordial, mango juice and ice and shake well.

3. Pour into 2 glasses. Pour on the grenadine.

Ginger Drink

Ingredients

Serves 2

4 inch / 10 cm piece fresh ginger root, coarsely grated (reserve juice)

2 tbsp brown sugar

1 large lemon

2 cups / 500 ml sparkling mineral water

Fresh mint sprigs, to garnish

Method

Prep and cook time: 30 min

1. Put the ginger and its juice into a pitcher and sprinkle in the sugar.

2. Zest and juice the lemon, then add the zest to the jug and mash with a pestle or with the tip of a rolling pin. Squeeze the lemon and add the juice to the pitcher.

3. Pour in the sparkling water. Allow to stand for 10 minutes; taste and add a little more sugar, if necessary.

4. Strain the ginger drink through a sieve into a pitcher. Divide between 2 glasses with lots of ice and some sprigs of mint.

INDEX